OUTSIDE THE GAME

OUTSIDE THE GAME

A COLLECTION
OF INSPIRATIONAL
SPORTS STORIES

JIM MANDELARO

 RIT PRESS   ROCHESTER, NEW YORK

RIT Press
90 Lomb Memorial Drive
Rochester, New York 14623-5604
http://ritpress.rit.edu

Book and cover design by Marnie Soom
Printed in the U.S.A.

All photos are used with permission from the Rochester *Democrat and Chronicle.*

ISBN 978-1-939125-15-6 (print)
ISBN 978-1-939125-16-3 (e-book)

Library of Congress Cataloging-in-Publication Data

Mandelaro, Jim.
    Outside the game : a collection of inspirational sports stories / Jim Mandelaro.
    pages   cm
    Includes index.
    ISBN 978-1-939125-15-6 (print : alk. paper) — ISBN 978-1-939125-16-3 (e-book)
    1. Sports—Miscellanea. 2. Sports—Biography. 3. Athletes—Biography.
    4. Sports—History. I. Title.
    GV707.M26 2015
    796—dc23

                                                                        2015006933

To Kerri, who changed my life. And to Matty and Sophie, who completed it.
To my mother, Connie Mandelaro, the most resilient woman I know.
And to my father-in-law, Bill Bishop (1935-2014),
who always loved a good story.

CONTENTS

PART 3: BEHIND THE SCENES

PART 4: FROM ALL WALKS OF LIFE

ACKNOWLEDGMENTS

The author wishes to acknowledge Bruce Austin, Lou Buttino, Frank Cardon, Tricia Cavalier, Molly Cort, the *Democrat and Chronicle*, Marie De Jesus, Jeff DiVeronica, Joanie Eppinga, Jamie Germano, Chuck Hinkel, Reed Hoffmann, Adrian Kraus, Annette Lein, Doug Mandelaro, Bob Matthews, Melissa Miller, John Maroon, Matt Michael, Jim Memmott, Kris Murante, Dennis O'Donnell, Carlos Ortiz, Tom Proietti, Mike Ryan, Max Schulte, Jim Seward, Marnie Soom and Will Yurman. Also, the late Tom Batzold, Bill Koenig and Rick Woodson, great journalists who helped make the old Rochester *Times-Union* one of the best sports sections in America.

INTRODUCTION

JUNE 15, 1999. I'M SITTING NEXT TO A LIVING SPORTS LEGEND IN a beautiful major-league baseball stadium, and I'm the only person allowed to talk to him. Nearly 20 reporters look on in frustration as I have this national icon all to myself.

This is my field of dreams.

I've driven south from Rochester, New York, where I work as a sportswriter for the *Democrat and Chronicle*, to Baltimore, Maryland. The Baltimore Orioles are coming to Rochester later this month to play their Triple-A affiliate, the Rochester Red Wings, in an annual exhibition, and I've decided to pursue an interview with Cal Ripken Jr., a future Hall of Famer whose big-league record streak of playing in 2,632 consecutive games ended the year before. Weeks before my trip, I contacted Orioles media relations director John Maroon about securing an interview with Ripken. But I don't want to write about The Streak, I tell him. "I want to write about Cal the person. I want to show what he does behind the scenes. I know he works with a lot of terminally ill children. This is a side of Cal that many don't see."

It's a side of Ripken that Maroon wants people to see, and he tells me he'll make it happen. I'm thrilled, of course, but I'm also concerned that my sensitive questions won't mesh with Ripken's usual pregame interrogations, such as: "What's wrong with the Orioles?" "What happened in the fifth inning last night?" "Why did you change your batting stance again?" I express these worries via email to Maroon, and his reply puts me at ease.

1

"Don't worry about it," he says. "I'll take care of you."

I have something of a history with Ripken, albeit a minor one. In July 1997, the Orioles were set to make their first visit to Frontier Field, which had opened for baseball three months earlier in downtown Rochester, to play the Red Wings. I was planning a trip to Cleveland for the Major League All-Star Game, but I didn't think it would go over well with the media contingent if I asked questions about Rochester on such a national stage. I asked Orioles media relations assistant Heather Tilles the best plan. "Just email me questions you want to ask Cal, and I'll make sure he sees them," she said. I do it. But I am not prepared for the response Heather delivers a few weeks later.

"Cal said he'll just call you."

Call me? He's Cal Ripken, and he's going to call me at my little condominium in Fairport, New York? The date and time are set, and he indeed calls — four hours before a game. He's articulate and open, and he doesn't make me feel rushed. I head to Cleveland, but my story is already written in my head.

Which leads me to my Baltimore visit two years later. I arrive at Camden Yards more than four hours before game time, hoping to catch Ripken before he starts preparing for another major-league baseball game. But he is nowhere to be found, a couple of hours pass, and I begin to worry. I know he soon will want to focus on the game, but the exhibition is looming, and this is my last night in Baltimore. The interview has to happen. And then, about an hour before the first pitch, it does. Ripken emerges into the dugout. I feel a lump in my throat.

"Jim," Maroon says, motioning to me. "Are you ready?"

As Ripken sits in the dugout, the throng of television, radio and newspaper reporters starts to converge on him. The big prize has arrived.

"Wait!" Maroon yells, as if removing visitors from a buffet line. "Only him." And he points to me. The media horde backs away, but they continue to stare, wondering who I am and how I was granted such special privileges.

Sports Illustrated? USA Today? New York Times?

No, just little ol' me. The interview proceeds, and while I am nervous at first, Ripken's easy-going manner puts me at ease once again. I find him thoughtful and introspective. I like him.

The story that comes out of that amazing interview is the first story in this book, a collection of human interest stories with a sports theme. Ripken is an amazing person. He is among the most famous baseball players ever to play the game, yet he constantly gives back. When Red Wings general manager Dan Mason informed the Ironman that he was being inducted into the team's Hall of Fame in 2003, Ripken had only one request: that he be allowed to host a free baseball clinic at Frontier Field the morning after the ceremony with his brother, former major-league infielder Billy Ripken. And he did, working for three hours one late-August morning with 60 youngsters from Rochester and the surrounding area.

Ripken is just one of the people in this book who inspire me – so much that he bookends this collection. He is the first and last person I write about.

But there are others here whose stories you may not know. They inspire me, too. And I hope they inspire you as well.

I've always held one primary goal as a writer: to evoke emotion. I want to make you laugh, cry — and think. I want to write the kind of human interest story that makes you say, "Gramma, you've got to read this." It doesn't matter if I'm writing about a Hall of Famer like Ripken or an eighth-grade football star named Rene Ingoglia (who would go on to play Division I football at the University of Massachusetts and cover games for ESPN). I want to know everything about my subject, and I want you to know, too. The canvas is blank before the interview starts. If I've done my job, it is full when my story is complete.

I've been a sportswriter for nearly 30 years, but I've always strived to write beyond the baseball diamond, basketball court or football field. Outside the game. Although working in Rochester doesn't get you up close and personal to the superstars of sports every day, you get some moments you'll never forget. Like O.J. Simpson waking you up from your sleep in 1991, two weeks after you've requested an interview, and three years before he goes from famous to infamous; or making a phone call to ESPN basketball analyst Dick Vitale in his Detroit hotel room at 7 a.m. (he picked the time); or "Prime Time" Deion Sanders (who played Major League Baseball and the National Football League *in the same week)* asking to speak to you in the clubhouse so that he could tell you that music you said he likes . . . well, he doesn't like it anymore. I've interviewed hundreds of people. At times, I've fallen victim to the stereotypes: *Pro athletes are hard to deal with, and baseball players are the worst. There's nothing better than talking to a high school or college athlete.* In reality, I've forged strong relationships with pro athletes like Chris Colabello, Doug Bernier and Jeff Manto, all of whom played major-league baseball, and international soccer star Abby Wambach. A few Division III athletes have refused to be interviewed, and I wonder what they're doing now.

My first writing assignment at the *Democrat and Chronicle* was in 1984, when I was still a part-timer. My task was to cover a local tennis championship. I thought I had headline news when a 13-year-old girl appeared on her way to the championship title. I sat in the bleachers and, while the match was in progress, I wrote up the story on my now-obsolete Radio Shack laptop – the one with the green screen that showed just three lines of type. Then, I watched with a sinking feeling in my stomach as the girl suffered an injury and was forced to withdraw. I suddenly had to scratch my story and write about the actual champion. That tennis match taught me two things: Expect the unexpected — and never write a story that hasn't happened yet.

This book is a selection of sports features that I wrote and published in the *Democrat and Chronicle.* You'll find stories about famous athletes such as Ripken, Wambach and Dwight Gooden. But you'll also read about everyday people who overcame adversity despite amazing odds. People like Joe Vicario, who endured 28 surgeries in his first 12 years on earth and became the student manager of the Rochester Institute of Technology men's hockey team. Or Jake Simmons, who lost his mother to a vicious disease and his father to prison, but who persevered to become Buffalo State's all-time leading basketball scorer. The player whose record he beat is former National Basketball Association All-Star Randy Smith.

How do I get these stories? Sometimes they drop into my lap. The Vicario story started with an email one morning from Joe Venniro, the Rochester Institute of Technology sports information director. Joe gave me the *Reader's Digest* version of why Vicario would make a great story, and I fell in love with it. Venniro arranged a meeting outside the RIT ice rink, and I talked to the man known as "Part-Time Joe" for more than an hour. I reached out to his mother by email and interviewed his head coach and the associate head coach. I spoke with the director of hockey operations who hired him. Then I was able to write about one of the most courageous people I've ever met. Sometimes, as in the cases of Ripken and Simpson, the story happens because I make it happen.

I'm a sportswriter by definition — I write about sports — but I've always tried to be a people writer first. I want to get to the heart of what makes each person tick. It's not easy getting people to confide in you after you've just met them, but by being honest with them and being a great listener, by putting the pen down and letting the tape roll, I gain their trust. They are telling me stories they want to be told.

You don't have to be a fan of sports to enjoy these stories — just a fan of resilient people. I hope you read these stories, and I hope your grandmother enjoys them, too. If I've done it right, these stories will make you laugh, cry — and think.

Outside the game.

Jim Mandelaro
November 2014

1

FAME, FORTUNE AND DREAMS

In three decades as a sports journalist, I've covered the gamut of athletics. From fishing derbies and local golf tournaments to the World Series, the Super Bowl, the NCAA basketball tournament and major golf tournaments. I've interviewed some of the most famous names in sports history. Here are my stories on a few of them.

CAL RIPKEN JR.:
AN IRONMAN WITH HEART

Published June 27, 1999

I traveled to Baltimore midway through the 1999 season for a one-on-one interview with baseball icon Cal Ripken Jr. prior to his appearance at Frontier Field for the Orioles' exhibition game against the Red Wings. This story focused on his charitable work, much of it behind the scenes.

IT'S 75 MINUTES BEFORE GAME TIME AND CAL RIPKEN JR. IS nowhere to be found. On the field at Oriole Park at Camden Yards, Baltimore Orioles coach Marv Foley throws batting practice while players stretch, field ground balls and shag flies. The clock on the right-field scoreboard ticks down toward the start of the game. But the only people who can be seen wearing No. 8 are the fans in the stands who have "Ripken" stitched on the backs of their Orioles shirts. The real Ripken is huddled in a private room at Camden Yards, meeting with a terminally ill child. The 8-year-old boy was asked what his greatest wish was, and he chose meeting his idol.

"I don't try to make a big deal out of it at all," Ripken says. "It's real simple to me. I recognized an opportunity a long time ago. As a baseball player, just by your actions and how you handle yourself, you can have an impact on some young person's life."

Ripken was merely a great player before September 6, 1995, when he became a national icon. On that date, he broke New York Yankees legend Lou Gehrig's hallowed record of playing in 2,130 consecutive major league games. Last September, the legendary third baseman pulled the plug on his streak at 2,632 games. The record run is over, but the same tune is played in every city. Ripken's marketing firm, The Tufton Group, will field requests from families and organizations representing sick children, and then work with Julie Wagner, the Orioles' community relations director, to set up meetings.

"The thing that amazes me is how good Cal is at it," says John Maroon, the Orioles' media relations director and one of Ripken's closest friends within the organization. "You get a 6-year-old kid that's going to be dead in a few months . . . that's a little too much reality for most athletes. Cal finds it uplifting and inspirational to see the courage these kids show."

Ripken is incredibly organized and regimented, but he makes time for those less fortunate. The routine goes something like this: Ripken plays with the children, asks what position they play, and often makes fun of himself by asking, "You wear No. 8?" He gets background information before the meetings, asking parents, "What's wrong with this child? What stage is he in?" Then he follows it up weeks later. Meeting with terminally ill children brings out deep emotions in Ripken — though not the type one might expect.

"Nine times out of 10, Julie will walk out of the room weeping, the parents will walk out bawling and Cal and the kid are in the room having a good time," Maroon says.

"Being a father of two drives it home a bit more," Ripken says. "I'm in a unique position being in the public eye, and I realize some positive can come from that. This isn't about me. It's about seeing a face light up and getting a positive reaction. The strength these children exhibit inspires me."

Ripken's compassion touched two Rochester-area families in 1997. Kyle Marchase was a 16-year-old boy from Honeoye Falls who idolized Ripken. By '97, Kyle was in a losing battle with non-Hodgkin's lymphoma. The Orioles visited Frontier Field that year, and the Red Wings set up a meeting between Kyle and baseball's ironman.

"Kyle was so excited," says Pat Knebel, whose son Rob was Kyle's best friend. "He'd had heavy doses of chemo. He was pretty weak and needed a wheelchair. But he said 'I'm not going to be in a wheelchair when I meet Cal Ripken.'"

Kyle pulled himself out of his wheelchair and showed Ripken the jersey Rob's family had given him — a Ripken jersey. Ripken put it on and modeled it, to Kyle's delight, then signed autographs and took photos with the boy.

"Cal was so wonderful," says Kyle's mother, Carol. "He didn't

*Cal Ripken, Jr. warms up before a 1997 exhibition against the
Rochester Red Wings at Frontier Field. Photographer: Jamie Germano*

rush us. He made jokes, he talked to all of us . . . He was great."

Nearly three months later — on November 22, 1997 — Ripken
was at a family party celebrating his daughter Rachel's eighth
birthday when he received a call from Rochester's Make-A-Wish
Foundation. Kyle had taken a drastic turn for the worse, and an official at Strong Memorial Hospital put the wheels in motion to track
Ripken down. Minutes later, the phone rang in Kyle's room. It was
Ripken. Kyle was too weak to talk, but Rob Knebel held a phone
to his friend's ear as Ripken spoke to his fan for the final time. The
future Hall of Famer talked about the day he'd met Kyle and how
much he had enjoyed it. Kyle simply listened.

"It was above and beyond anything we expected," Carol Marchase says. "Just wonderful."

Kyle died that day. The Marchase and Knebel families met privately with Ripken soon after to present him with a plaque that honored his "warmth and kindness." Ripken has endured much personal trauma this year. In March, his father died of lung cancer. On Opening Day, the still-grieving Ripken aggravated a back injury and had to leave the game. His play deteriorated. When he made two errors in one play against the New York Yankees, *Sports Illustrated* dubbed him "Iron Hands." But he bounced back and showed that he still has something left.

"He's done so many incredible things in his career," says Orioles shortstop Mike Bordick. "Seeing how fans appreciate that is great."

Bordick says the Orioles are "amazed" by how effortlessly Ripken deals with his fame and the demands on his time.

"The way he handles himself is incredible," he says. "When you look at someone like that, it makes you take a good look at yourself. You want to work harder for him."

Foley, who managed the Red Wings the previous four seasons, says Ripken is just one of the guys off the field.

"The fans see this national icon," Foley says. "We see a regular guy who's a lot of fun to be around."

Red Wings infielder P.J. Forbes met Ripken last summer after being promoted from Rochester.

"He finished taking batting practice and I was taking grounders," Forbes recalled. "He made a point of coming over to shake my hand and say 'Welcome aboard.' He didn't have to do that."

Ripken's mystique evokes admiration that extends beyond that of the average fan. Wings pitcher Darin Blood remembers the first time Ripken entered the clubhouse at the Orioles' minor-league complex, Twin Lakes Park in Sarasota, Florida, in May to begin a three-day rehabilitation stint.

"Guys were nudging each other saying, 'Look who it is!' and the other player would look and go 'Awesome!'"

"The fans were bad enough," Blood says. "They formed a long line beginning at 7 a.m., even though Cal didn't arrive until 9. But the young players were really in awe. When he left, Cal autographed balls for everyone."

The Orioles' two exhibitions against the Red Wings sold out in hours, and Wings general manager Dan Mason can spell out the reason in three letters.

"Cal is one of the most gracious athletes I've ever seen," he says. "He has an amazing presence, especially with kids."

Ripken played 114 consecutive games for the Red Wings in 1981 — including a 33-inning marathon against Pawtucket that remains the longest in pro baseball history — before his call-up to the Orioles that August. It was a modest streak that foreshadowed the record that would change his life.

"Rochester holds a lot of special memories for me," says Ripken, who earned International League Rookie of the Year honors in 1981. "It was the first time I actually felt good about coming to the big leagues. Going back there always brings back good memories. The easiest thing you can do to make someone happy is sign a ball or piece of paper."

Forbes says it's easy to understand why fans love Ripken.

"He's phenomenal," Forbes says. "He's not only a great player, he's total class. He's what every player should strive to be."

AN IRON-CLAD HALL OF FAMER

Cal Ripken Jr. retired in 2001 having made the All-Star team 19 times (he was Most Valuable Player twice). He was the 1982 American League Rookie of the Year in 1982 and the MVP in 1983 and '91.

Ripken finished his illustrious career with 3,184 hits, 431 home runs and 1,695 runs batted in. And his record of playing in 2,632 consecutive games most certainly will never be broken.

In 2007, Ripken was elected to the Baseball Hall of Fame, receiving 98.53 percent of the vote, the third-largest ever.

HOWARD BINGHAM:
PHOTOGRAPHS AND MEMORIES

Published January 25, 1999

As chief photographer to Muhammad Ali, the most famous man on the planet, Howard Bingham has been everywhere and seen just about everything. He has described himself as the "Forrest Gump of photojournalism"—popping up at just the right moment to photograph some of sports' greatest moments. This article was published the week he appeared at the Rochester Press-Radio Club dinner in 1999 to accept the first Kodak Vision Award. But even when he was being honored for a lifetime of photographic excellence, Bingham was upstaged by his best friend. Headliner David Wells of the New York Yankees never showed up at the dinner. Bingham tipped off Ali, and the greatest legend in boxing history flew in and stunned the crowd by walking onstage, bringing down the house by cupping his hand to his ear and saying, "David Who?"

"When Muhammad Ali is on his deathbed, chances are he will rise up on one elbow, look around and demand, 'Where's Howard?' Howard will be right there."

– Jim Murray in *Muhammad Ali: A Thirty-Year Journey.*

HOWARD BINGHAM MAY BE THE MOST FAMOUS PERSON YOU'VE never heard of. He has met presidents, princes, dictators — and a King named Elvis Presley. He has been on the cover of *Sports Illustrated* and was a witness in the "trial of the century." At home in Los Angeles, he's a frequent flier on Bill Cosby's private jet. In Rochester, he thinks nothing of hugging Eastman Kodak Company CEO George Fisher – or sitting in Fisher's chair, pounding his fist on the desk and kiddingly promising to "turn this company around." And his best friend, Ali, might be the world's most recognized person.

"It all leaves me speechless," Bingham says. "I have to pinch myself. I can't believe it."

For 36 years, Bingham has been Ali's confidant, companion, and relentless photographer. Ali has been part of the nation's consciousness for four decades, and Bingham has recorded the times of his life every step of the way.

"He made me," Bingham says, "and I made him."

And then he laughs.

Bingham was born in Jackson, Mississippi, but moved to Los Angeles at age 4 and has lived there ever since. Bingham's father was a minister with strict values. To this day, Howard doesn't know how to dance. "My parents didn't allow it," he says.

Bingham attended Compton College, outside of Los Angeles, and majored in music. He received Fs in several classes, including one in photography.

"I was young, dumb and having fun," he explains. He worked two years mopping floors and moving stock before deciding to follow in the footsteps of his neighbors and become a photographer, mainly so that he could meet young women. He earned an internship at the *Los Angeles Sentinel,* one of the nation's largest black newspapers, and in 1962 was assigned to cover a brash young boxer from Louisville named Cassius Clay, who had won an Olympic gold medal in 1960 and was in town to promote a fight.

"I'd never heard of him before," Bingham says. "Cassius who?"

Bingham photographed the event and left. But later that day, he spotted Clay and his brother, Rudolph Valentino Clay, while driving through Los Angeles.

"I pulled over and asked them what they were doing," he says, "and they said, 'Looking for girls.'"

Bingham offered to show the brothers around town, and after hours of sightseeing he took them to his mother's house for a home-cooked meal. The bond was formed. Whenever Clay arrived in Los Angeles, he hooked up with Bingham. Clay became a Muslim, changed his name to Ali and became a boxing legend and an international icon. And Bingham kept clicking away. In Europe, Africa, Asia and everywhere across the globe. Nearly four decades later, he's still clicking.

During the turbulent 1960s, Bingham landed jobs with several

Muhammad Ali made a surprise appearance at the 1999 Rochester Press-Radio Club dinner, joining old friend Howard Bingham at the podium at the Rochester Convention Center. Bingham was being honored with the Eastman Kodak Vision Award. Photographer: Reed Hoffmann

national magazines, including a five-year stint with *Life*, for which he traveled the country and photographed the endless urban riots. The Black Panthers trusted Bingham enough to let him photograph their huge weapons cache. But through it all, Bingham covered Ali. When Ali married for the third time, Bingham was best man — and went on the honeymoon. He was there for the highs and the lows, ultimately putting his work into the 1993 book *Muhammad Ali: A Thirty-Year Journey*. He has remained with "The Greatest" through Ali's long bout with Parkinson's disease. But Bingham is not at Ali's side.

"I like walking behind him," he says with a laugh. "Watching as people walk toward him. They think they're seeing things."

The scenario is the same wherever they go.

"The people don't believe it," says Bingham, 59. "They run into the airport gift shop and get a Kodak throwaway camera and they run after Ali, hoping for a chance to get his autograph or get a picture taken with him. And Ali signs for everyone. We miss a lot of planes."

Through his association with Ali, Bingham has visited dozens of countries and every continent. He recently traveled to Australia for the first time and snorkeled.

"And I don't even swim!" he says.

Ali is better off than people think, Bingham says.

"The media makes it worse. He is not like he used to be, but his mind is 100 percent. Ali loves to do magic tricks. He loves to eat fattening foods, like ice cream and cake. He's on the road all the time, busier than ever."

Ali lives with his fourth wife, Lonnie, on an 88-acre farm in Berrien Springs, Michigan. Bingham, divorced and with two grown sons, is in daily contact with the Alis and saw the former champ recently for the Mike Tyson-Francois Botha fight in Las Vegas. Why does the graceful Ali still support the enigmatic Tyson?

"Mike has always idolized Ali," Bingham explains. "When Mike was in jail (for rape), Ali wanted to visit but Mike said no. He didn't want Ali to see him in that position. But when he got out, Ali was there to greet him."

Ali believes there is good in everyone and that Tyson is vulnerable to bad influences, Bingham says.

"Ali can't turn his back on anyone. He can only do what he thinks is right and hope for the best."

You might say Bingham carries a torch for Ali. He proved it at the 1996 Summer Olympics in Atlanta, when he began a process that ended with Ali lighting the flame to open the Games.

"I lobbied for it a long time," he says. "Olympic officials, people in Atlanta, (NBC president) Dick Ebersol. Everyone."

Bingham knew about the selection but didn't tell Ali until a few days before the event.

"He can't keep a secret," Bingham says. "And the Atlanta people didn't want anyone to find out."

Even President Clinton was kept in the dark. Minutes after Ali lit the torch, Clinton put his hands on Ali's shoulders and told him,

"They did not tell me who was going to light the flame. When I saw it was you, I cried."

Bingham calls Ali "Bill," and Ali calls Bingham "Bill." The name means nothing, the symbolism everything: They are on even ground. Bingham is unassuming, jovial, and an admitted "wise guy."

An interviewer asks, "Have you been to Rochester, Mr. Bingham?"

"What, Rochester, Minnesota?" he says, laughing loudly.

Actually, Bingham is a frequent visitor here in Rochester, New York. Ali's management group, IMG, is based in New York and Bingham often stops here on his way home. He has become close friends with Fisher and his wife Ann, Kodak President/chief operating officer Dan Carp, and Roger Strong, a service engineer in marketing support at Kodak. Bingham and Strong met in 1994, when Ali visited Rochester for a tribute to former heavyweight boxer George Chuvalo. The two became fast friends and speak almost daily.

"He'll call me just to play messages," Strong says. "One was from Warren Beatty, inviting him to dinner."

Last August, Bingham insisted on paying for lunch during a visit to Rochester. Strong secretly put a $10 bill into his bag with a note that said "Gotcha!" Bingham never mentioned it, but a few weeks ago, the Strong family was en route to Hawaii when they ran into Bingham in Los Angeles.

"You must have some food in there," Bingham told Strong's two children, as he began rifling through their backpacks.

"When we unpacked, we saw he had stuck an envelope with 10 bucks in each backpack," Strong says. "And there was a note: 'Gotcha back!'"

Despite his friendship with the rich and famous — he's even tight with Senator Orrin Hatch of Utah — Bingham lives modestly in a three-bedroom home in South Los Angeles he has owned since 1969. He seemingly knows everyone, talking daily with, for example, Camille Cosby, Bill's wife. When Bingham ran for Congress in 1978, his supporters included Marvin Gaye, Sammy Davis Jr., Richard Pryor and Ali, who wrote a poem:

Bingham is smart
Bingham is wise
Elect Howard Bingham
Cut our problems down to size.

Bingham lost the race.

When the Cosbys' son, Ennis, was murdered in 1997, Bingham made the funeral arrangements. When he was honored as Photographer of the Year by the Photographic Marketing Distribution Association last year, he dedicated the award to Ennis. Bingham is so well known at LAX that airport officials watch his car. On June 12, 1994, he was on a redeye to Chicago when he ran into football legend O.J. Simpson.

"I was sitting in coach, getting ready to lie down," he says. "I've known O.J. since 1968, and I got up to say hello. We talked for a minute, then we talked again after the plane landed. I saw nothing unusual."

That brief meeting led to Bingham's being called as a witness in Simpson's murder trial following the brutal deaths of his ex-wife Nicole Brown Simpson and her friend, Ronald Goldman. Bingham was widely described as "the only witness both sides liked."

Johnnie Cochran (approaching Bingham): "Are you a world-renowned photographer?"

Bingham: "The world's greatest."

Later, Judge Lance Ito jokingly referred to Bingham as the "world's greatest" photographer.

"You're a smart man, judge," Bingham said, drawing laughter from the jury, the judge and the world-famous defendant.

So, is O.J. guilty?

"I wasn't there," Bingham says.

He has not seen Simpson since the trial.

Bingham's calendar is full, but he made time to receive the Vision Award in Rochester. It means a great deal to him.

"To receive this award in the city that's the home of the major photographic giant is huge," he says. "It is a big, big honor."

He could pinch himself.

BOBBY GRICH AND DON BAYLOR: BASEBALL SOULMATES

Published August 9, 2010

Bobby Grich and Don Baylor were the heart and soul of arguably the greatest Rochester Red Wings team of all time, the 1971 Junior World Series champions. Both went on to enjoy successful big-league careers, and Baylor was named 1979 American League Most Valuable Player. Four decades after that great '71 season, the former baseball stars returned to Rochester, New York, for their joint induction into the International League Hall of Fame.

YOU CAN FORGIVE BOBBY GRICH IF HE CRINGED THE FIRST 20 times he heard Don Baylor's name. Grich was the Baltimore Orioles' first-round draft pick in 1967. Baylor was the Orioles' second-round selection.

"I negotiated with them for almost a month, trying to raise my bonus," Grich recalls, "and the scouts kept using Don Baylor as a negotiating ploy. They'd say: 'We weren't even sure we wanted to draft you. We wanted to make sure we got Don Baylor.'"

To which Grich replied: "Maybe you should have drafted Baylor first."

Grich had been offered a full scholarship to play quarterback at UCLA, but he wanted to play baseball. Baylor also could have gone the football route, but University of Texas coach Darrell Royal wouldn't let him play both sports. Grich was 18, and Baylor was 17. Grich finally signed and reported to the Orioles' rookie-level club in Bluefield, West Virginia.

"The first player to come up to me was Donnie Baylor, with a big smile on his face," Grich recalls. "He said: 'I'm Donnie Baylor, welcome to the team.' From that moment on, we were best friends, with no animosities."

Grich would rise through the Orioles system as a star shortstop, and right alongside him was Baylor, an outfielder with power and speed. They would be teammates for all but one season from 1967-82, from the low minors to the major league playoffs and spanning two organizations. Along the way, they would share the spotlight as the leaders of arguably the greatest Red Wings team ever, the 1971 Junior World Series champions.

"I always think of Bobby Grich and Don Baylor in the same breath," says their longtime minor league manager, Joe Altobelli, who guided the Red Wings from 1971-76. "All of my other years in Rochester kind of blend together, but '71 stands out. It was special, and much of it was because of Grich and Baylor."

In the late 1960s, racial prejudice was alive and not-so-well in America, especially the Southern states. Baylor felt it, and Grich hurt for him. "I remember being in Bluefield in '67 and black guys had to stay at a certain apartment building," Grich says. "One time we were on a bus trip — it was either Salem, Virginia, or Johnson City, Tennessee — and we pulled off the highway to eat a meal. The proprietor said something to Alto (then the Bluefield manager) that they wouldn't serve black players. So the whole team got back on the bus and went to another restaurant."

After failing to find anyone in Bluefield who would rent their house or apartment, Baylor and fellow African-American teammates Herman Grant and Lew Beasley stayed at a local hotel for $100 per month.

"There were two real good beds and one cot," Baylor remembers. "We always gave the pitcher (Grant) one of the good beds. Then the other bed went to whoever got the most hits that day, Lew or me. I ended up hitting .346 and won the batting title."

Grich also remembers how the city of Bluefield would hold a teenage dance on Friday nights, a square dance on Saturday nights — and a "black dance" on Sunday nights.

"Blacks weren't really allowed to go to the other dances," he says.

Through it all, they were best friends: Grich, the white infielder from Long Beach, California, and Baylor, the black outfielder from Austin, Texas.

"In 1972, we roomed together in Baltimore and I think we were

the first black and white teammates to room together in the majors,"
Grich says.

Baylor married in 1970, and Grich tied the knot one year later.
Although both have since remarried, in those days they went out as
couples all the time. The players were so close that Grich is godfa-
ther to Baylor's son, Don Jr., born in 1972. Grich and Baylor played
together for Bluefield in 1967, Stockton in '68, Dallas-Fort Worth
in '69 and Rochester in '70 and '71. Baylor was named *The Sporting
News'* Minor League Player of the Year in 1970. Grich earned the
honor the next year, when the Wings recorded that season to remember. Grich and Baylor felt they had proven themselves at Triple-A in
1970 and were ready for the big time. One problem: The Orioles, in
the midst of a three-year World Series run, were loaded with stars.
Frank Robinson, Don Buford and Paul Blair in the outfield. Mark
Belanger at shortstop. When the Orioles finalized their roster out of
spring training, they sent Grich and Baylor to Rochester. They were
not happy campers that spring.

"I told (Orioles general manager) Harry Dalton I was going to go
home and think about it for a while," Baylor says. "Harry called and
said: 'We know both of you guys can play in the majors, but there's
no room for you.' It was disappointing for both of us."

They agreed to return. Rochester began the year 0-5 and was
still an underachieving 33-33 in June. But then the Wings caught
fire. Behind Grich, Baylor and star pitcher Roric Harrison, they went
53-21 down the stretch. They captured the Governors' Cup title,
awarded to the International League champions, and then outlasted
the Denver Bears in seven games to win the Junior World Series title.
All seven games were played at Rochester's Silver Stadium due to a
stadium scheduling conflict in Denver.

"It was fantastic," Baylor says. "We reigned supreme. At the time,
I didn't know I would play in three straight World Series (1986-88).
This was our world championship."

Grich calls that summer "the most fun I've ever had in baseball."

He says, "We didn't have BlackBerries, laptops and things like
that. We had each other on those long bus trips."

Grich was promoted to the Orioles after Game 5 of the Junior

World Series. This time, he didn't want to go.

"I wanted to finish what I started in Rochester," he says.

The Wings were stunned by the move.

"How could they take him away from us at that time?" Baylor says. "He wanted to stay. But when Earl Weaver calls, you go."

The Wings lost Game 6, making them 0-12 without Grich in the lineup. He had missed all of those games because of Army Reserve obligations. Rochester outlasted Denver 9-6 to win Game 7, stamping that 1971 club as arguably the greatest in franchise history. Grich led the International League with a .336 average and 32 home runs. He scored 124 runs and drove in 83.

After '71, the two would never again play in the minors. Grich was shifted to second base in Baltimore and became a premier player. Baylor manned left field and also became a star. The Orioles reached the playoffs in 1973 and '74 but were done in both times by the Oakland A's dynasty. The Dynamic Duo had played together for nine straight seasons, from Bluefield to Baltimore, but it came to a shocking end on April 2, 1976. Baylor was dealt to Oakland in a deal involving megastar Reggie Jackson. Baylor cried that night in the Orioles' spring training clubhouse in Miami. "How," he asked a friend, "am I going to tell Bobby?"

Grich was crushed.

"An era had closed," he says. "For the first time in nine years, I was going to be without my close friend. It was sad. Before that trade, Donnie and I envisioned playing our entire careers with the Orioles, just like Brooks Robinson."

They wouldn't be apart for long.

"A new thing called free agency was coming on board," Grich says.

When the 1976 season ended, Grich and Baylor both became free agents. At the time, teams could sign only as many players as they lost via free agency. For the California Angels, that meant three.

"I was very interested in playing for the Angels, since I lived in Long Beach," Grich says.

While traveling home from Baltimore, he learned that the Angels had signed Baylor and outfielder Joe Rudi as free agents.

"I was thrilled," he says. "I called my agent (Jerry Kapstein) and told him: 'Make it happen, Jerry. I want to play for the Angels.'"

Kapstein told Grich he had bad news.

"Mr. (Gene) Autry said he's done signing free agents," Kapstein told him. "That's all the money he wants to spend."

Grich was stunned.

"He's got a chance to sign three free agents, and he needs a short-stop," he told Kapstein. "How can they not sign me? Tell Mr. Autry I'll sign for the first offer they made me last month. I want to go to California."

The Yankees were offering Grich more money than the Angels. But Grich was insistent. When he arrived in Long Beach, he called Kapstein again. This time, his agent had good news.

"Mr. Autry said if you want to play for the Angels that bad, he'll sign you," Kapstein told him.

Grich laughs at the memory.

"I had to freaking beg him to sign me," he says.

The contract was worth $1.5 million for five years.

Grich and Baylor were together again. They would be team-mates on the Angels through 1982, and in that final year the Angels won the American League West before falling to the Milwaukee Brewers in the playoffs. During the offseason, it was Baylor who signed a free-agent deal with the Yankees. The two would never play together again, but they would be on opposite sides of one of the most memorable postseason games in baseball history.

In 1986, Grich's Angels met Baylor's Red Sox in the American League championship series. The Angels had never reached the World Series, but that seemed imminent when Grich drove in another former Red Wing, Jerry Narron, in the bottom of the 11th of Game 4 to give the Angels a 3 games to 1 lead. They needed one more win to stamp their ticket to the Fall Classic.

"We were going to the World Series," Grich says. "We were convinced."

In Game 5, Grich homered to put the Angels up 3-2 in the sixth inning, and that lead increased to 5-2.

But in the ninth, Baylor hit a two-run homer and Dave Henderson followed with a memorable two-run shot off Donnie

Moore to put Boston ahead. Rob Wilfong tied the game in the bottom half with a single, but Henderson's sacrifice fly in the 11th scored Baylor with what proved to be the winning run. Boston trounced the deflated Angels in the final two games, winning 10-4 and 8-1 to win the series.

"It was the most physically draining series I've ever been part of," Baylor says.

After Game 7, Grich announced his retirement.

"I'd had enough," he says. "I was finished."

He hit .266 with 224 home runs and 864 RBI in a 17-season career that included six All-Star appearances and four Gold Gloves.

Baylor would become the first player in major league history to reach the World Series in three consecutive years with three different teams (Boston in '86, Minnesota in '87 and Oakland in '88). He retired after the '88 season with a .260 average, 338 homers and 1,276 RBI.

All these years later, Grich and Baylor talk about once a month and see each other a few times each year.

"It's funny that we're such good friends," Grich says. "He doesn't play golf much, and I'm an avid golfer. He stayed in the game, and I didn't. The only thing we have in common is baseball and our history."

When Baylor learned he was going into the International League Hall of Fame, his first question was: "Is Grich included in that?"

He is, and for the first time in 35 years, the heart and soul of '71 will be in Rochester together.

"We were a tandem in Rochester," Baylor says. "Forever, really."

JIM NANTZ: LIVING THE DREAM

Published July 31, 2003

As roommates and golf teammates at the University of Houston in the late 1970s, Jim Nantz and Fred Couples would often hold practice interviews after Couples had "won" the Masters Tournament. Nantz would pretend to interview Couples on capturing golf's most prestigious title. And then, years later, it happened for real. Nantz recounted that improbable dream come true during a visit to Oak Hill Country Club in Rochester before the 2003 PGA Championship.

BY HIS FRESHMAN YEAR AT THE UNIVERSITY OF HOUSTON IN 1977, Jim Nantz realized he was on a divergent career path from his roommate and golf teammate, Fred Couples.

"I wanted to work for CBS Sports," Nantz says, "and Freddie wanted to be a professional golfer. The goals were clearly defined."

In an effort to improve his skills as a journalist and prepare his pals for impending stardom on the PGA Tour, Nantz often would practice interviewing Couples and his other roommate, former PGA Tour member Blaine McCallister, in their dorm room.

"I sold them on the fact that they were going to have to learn how to handle the media," Nantz said. "And so into a large tape deck, and with a stick microphone, I would interview them. With Freddie, the scenario was always the same: Butler Cabin, Augusta, Georgia. I was the host for CBS Sports, and he was the champion. And I was there to present him with the green jacket."

Fantasy became reality on April 12, 1992, when Couples won the Masters over Ray Floyd and Corey Pavin, capturing his first major championship.

"I had this awkward feeling all day," Nantz said. "I had this uneasy feeling that I was going to lose my emotions."

At the 17th hole, CBS analyst Ben Wright asked Nantz what was going through his mind.

"I had a hard time getting the words out," Nantz said. "My voice was quivering on the air."

Nantz realized he had to keep his composure, but it was hard. Couples had remained one of his best friends, and the realization of what was happening seemed overwhelming.

Couples entered the cabin after his victory, and the two friends barely looked at each other. They continued to avoid each other, amazingly, through the entire interview on live TV.

"If you go back and look at the tape you'll see that I'm directly across from Fred," Nantz said. "Every time the camera was on him, he was shielding his eyes with his hands so he wouldn't look at me."

Cameraman Dave Finch recorded the emotional interview.

"It was very special because you saw two very special friends finally have a dream come true," Finch said. "We all knew they had rehearsed it in college, and here it was playing out in real life."

Unbeknownst to Nantz and Couples, Finch let the tape keep rolling after the show went off the air.

What he captured was an April shower of the most humane kind. "We finished the interview and as soon as I said goodbye, the two of us completely lost it," Nantz said. "Little did I know the cameras were rolling."

They were tears of joy, and of a dream come true.

ABBY WAMBACH: FAMILY TIES

Published September 16, 2001

*Before she became an international soccer star, Abby Wambach
revealed that her real heroes growing up were the kids she lived with:
her brothers and sisters. When this story was published—the week of
the terrorist attacks on America—the University of Florida senior
had just been named to the U.S. national team.*

GROWING UP IN PITTSFORD, NEW YORK, ABBY WAMBACH'S
heroes weren't sports stars such as Michael Jordan, John Elway and
Mia Hamm. Her idols were named Beth, Laura, Peter, Matthew,
Patrick and Andrew — her six older brothers and sisters.

"It was so easy for me to have that outlet where I could ask questions," Wambach says. "My idols were living at home."

Abby grilled her siblings about "stupid stuff" such as what it felt
like to score a goal or win a match.

Either they were great teachers or she was a great student — or
both — because Abby has reached heights that other soccer players
only dream about.

Last week, Wambach was named to the United States women's
national team, joining the 18-person roster. Wambach played 14 minutes in a 4-1 Nike U.S. Cup win against Germany last Sunday, but
games against Japan and China were canceled because of the terrorist attacks in New York City and Washington, D.C. Wambach
returned to the University of Florida this weekend. Making the
national team is just the latest honor in a resume that seems to grow
at the rate she scores goals.

She was named National High School Player of the Year as a
senior in 1997 and Southeastern Conference Player of the Year at
Florida as a junior in 2000. She was the leading scorer on the U.S.
Under-21 team that won the Nordic Cup in 2001. A few weeks later,
she was named to the United States National Team, joining soccer

*Rochester native
Abby Wambach
scores the first goal
with a header as the
United States beat
Iceland at Frontier
Field in 2004.
Photographer:
Will Yurman*

superstars such as Hamm and Brandi Chastain. Wambach is on a
fast track to accomplishing one of the few goals she has yet to realize:
carrying the torch that Hamm and Co. eventually will pass to a new
generation of soccer stars.

Florida coach Becky Burleigh, whose Gators won the 1998
national championship in Wambach's freshman year, says her high-
scoring forward doesn't remind her of any of today's current stars.

"She's got such a big frame (5-feet-11) and good speed," Burleigh
says. "Add in her competitiveness and she's really a trailblazer."

Wambach's sisters played soccer at Our Lady of Mercy High
School in Rochester — Laura went on to play four years at Division I
Xavier University — and her brothers played at McQuaid Jesuit and
Pittsford Sutherland. They tutored her about soccer and also taught
her to swim and play baseball. Wambach has always been ahead of

the game. At 2, she was riding a two-wheeled bicycle down her family's driveway. When she was 3, Mercy coach Kathy Boughton saw her playing in the gym and joked, "Boy, it's too bad I'm not going to be around when she comes through Mercy."

Boughton was around, all right. She coached Abby for five varsity seasons in soccer and four in basketball.

When Wambach was 9, she left her girls youth soccer team after one season and joined the boys for the next five years. She played varsity soccer for five years and varsity basketball for four. Aquinas girls soccer coach Gary Page once was asked the key to beating Mercy.

"If Wambach would go on vacation one of these days, that would be nice," he said. She was entering her sophomore year at the time.

Wambach scored a school-record 142 goals for Mercy, but it was stopping a goal that ranks as her high school highlight. Mercy was leading Greece Athena 3-2 in the 1995 Section V Class A championship when Athena's Paula Listrani lined up for a penalty kick with 1:23 remaining. Boughton pulled her goalie and inserted Wambach, then a sophomore, explaining, "Abby's the best athlete in Rochester and she's great under pressure. You've got to go with your money player." Wambach had never played goalie before, but she made the save — and scored two goals — as Mercy won the title before about 500 chilled fans.

"That was awesome," she says.

Wambach is one of the greatest scorers in the college ranks, but she's all about her team.

"The happiest and most excited I've ever seen her was when Florida won the national championship," her mom, Judy, says.

Abby's idea of relaxing is watching *Beverly Hills 90210* reruns, hanging out with friends and listening to the Dave Matthews Band. And don't even think about calling her cell phone — she doesn't have one.

"I'm very much against cell phones," she says. "I had one for a month and had to get rid of it. Too many people were calling me."

Wambach didn't find out she had been invited to tryouts for the national team until she returned from Europe, where she played with the Gators.

*The Washington Freedom's Abby Wambach signs autographs for fans
after a 2003 game against the New York Power at Frontier Field.
Photographer: Carlos Ortiz*

"I got the Gainesville paper and there was an article about it," she
says. "I thought, 'Is someone playing a joke on me?'"

No joke. That week, Wambach joined Hamm, Chastain and the
rest of the national team in Chicago. Was she nervous? Was she
intimidated?

"No," she says. "They're exceptional soccer players, and they
deserve everything they've gotten. But I've never been in awe of
celebrities. They have to eat three times a day and sleep just like
everyone else."

Judy and Peter Wambach were driving to Chicago to see their
youngest child and learn if Abby had made the national team. Their
cell phone rang at around 1:30 p.m.

"She said 'I made it,' very calmly," her mother says.

Judy and Peter were not so calm.

"We had just entered Illinois, and we went crazy on Route 57, high-fiving each other," Judy says.

Then Judy started calling the other six children, the ones who had helped raise a rising star.

"They had all called me at least twice that morning to find out if Abby made it," Judy says. "They were on pins and needles. When they found out, everyone was so excited."

DWIGHT GOODEN: WINS AND LOSSES

Published July 27, 2013

Dwight Gooden burst onto the baseball scene as a New York Mets rookie in the mid-1980s, winning 17 games in 1984 and 24 in '85. His future seemed limitless. But a losing battle with drugs and alcohol cost him a spot in the Hall of Fame and shortened his career. He visited Rochester in 2013.

DWIGHT GOODEN KNOWS WHAT YOU'RE THINKING. HE TRADED IN a Hall of Fame baseball career for booze and drugs. His arrest record overwhelmed his win-loss record. He threw fame away as fast as he dealt his devastating fastball for the New York Mets in the mid-1980s. But Gooden would like you to know he's quite fine with his baseball résumé. He's happy with his 194 wins, his four All-Star Game appearances, his three World Series rings, his Rookie of the Year and Cy Young awards and, most especially, his no-hitter for the Yankees in 1996.

"I'm not ashamed of my career," he says. "I'm very proud of it."

Gooden isn't blind to his past, however. "I want people to know," he says, "that there's a better way."

Gooden grew up in Tampa an avid fan of the Cincinnati Reds, who trained there each spring. His baseball idols included Pete Rose, Tom Seaver and flamethrower Nolan Ryan. Gooden's rise to greatness was rapid. He was selected by the Mets with the fifth overall pick in the 1982 draft and spent just one full season in the minors, going 19-4 for Single-A Lynchburg in 1983. He struck out 300 batters in 191 innings. In 1984, he leapfrogged to the Mets and was named National League Rookie of the Year after winning 17 games — the most by a 19-year-old in 20 years. His 98 mph fastball and sweeping curveball led to a National League-best 276 strikeouts and the nickname "Dr. K," later shortened to just "Doc." To this day, he introduces himself as "Doc Gooden."

In 1985, Gooden crafted one of the most dominating seasons by any pitcher in baseball history, going 24-4 with a 1.53 earned-run average and a whopping 16 complete games. In his four losses, his earned-run average was a mere 2.89. In September, he tossed back-to-back nine-inning shutouts and received no-decisions each time.

"I was blown away by my numbers the first two years," he says. "I was happy just to make the team. Even today, when I look at those 1985 numbers, I'm amazed I was able to do that at such a young age. You'll probably never see that again."

In 1986, the Mets staged a miraculous rally in Game 6 of the World Series and went on to stun the Boston Red Sox in a seven-game thriller. Gooden's first call was to his father. His second call was to his dealer.

"I was in total denial," he says.

He missed the victory parade. As he writes in his new memoir, *Doc*, he woke up in a housing project on Long Island, zapped from a vodka and cocaine hangover. He watched the parade through New York's Canyon of Heroes on television and cried.

"That's when I knew I was powerless to stop this disease," he says.

The freefall continued two months later when he was arrested in Tampa after fighting with police. A report clearing police of misconduct helped start the Tampa riots of 1987. Gooden then tested positive for cocaine during spring training of '87 and entered a rehab center to avoid being suspended by Major League Baseball. Although he didn't pitch until June, he still won 15 games. The next year, he won 18. He was 21 and owner of 58 major-league victories entering 1987. But substance abuse continued to take its toll. In 1992, he finished 10-13. The next year, he was 12-15. *Sports Illustrated* ran a cover story on him called "From Phenom to Phantom."

It's easy to blame drugs and alcohol as the culprits, but Gooden also suffered from a heavy workload. It's estimated he threw nearly 11,000 pitches before his 20th birthday. Gooden tested positive again for cocaine in the strike-shortened 1994 season and was suspended for 60 days. He tested positive while serving the suspension and was suspended for the entire 1995 season. The day after he received that sentence, his wife, Monica, found Gooden in their bedroom with a loaded gun to his head. Gooden doesn't believe playing in New York City led him down his tortuous path.

"It could have happened anywhere," he says. "It was me making bad decisions and not putting myself in healthy situations."

Gooden signed with the Yankees as a free agent in 1996 and turned in what he calls the proudest achievement of his career on May 14 when he no-hit the Seattle Mariners at Yankee Stadium. His father had been on dialysis for 15 years due to kidney failure and his health was rapidly deteriorating. Doctors told the elder Gooden he needed open-heart surgery but weren't sure he would pull through.

"I thought about going home (to Tampa), but then I remembered all the times he took me to see Reds spring training games and all the games we listened to on the radio," Dwight Gooden says. "I knew he would want me to pitch. And that night (against the Mariners), I pitched as hard as I could."

Hard enough to make history.

The next morning, Gooden flew home and gave his father the game ball. His dad underwent surgery, went on life support and never made it home from the hospital. He died in January 1997, and Dwight's no-hitter was the last game he saw.

"That game will always be the greatest moment of my career, for what it meant to my dad," Gooden says.

He pitched for the Indians, Astros and Devil Rays from 1998 to 2000 and was unconditionally released twice before signing a minor-league deal with the Yankees. He returned to New York in 2000 but made only five starts and ended his career as a mop-up reliever for the World Series champions. He didn't pitch in the Subway Series against the Mets, but still received his third world championship ring. He retired in 2001 after being cut by the Yankees in spring training. His career mark was 194-112, and more than half of his wins came before he was 25. Five years later, he appeared on the National Baseball Hall of Fame ballot and received only 3.3 percent of the vote, which removed him from future consideration.

Gooden tried to stay in baseball, working in the Yankees' front office and later for the Newark Bears of the independent Atlantic League. But his demons kept following him, and his arrests kept mounting: DWI. Misdemeanor battery. Violating probation. Leaving the scene of an accident and endangering the welfare of a child. That last incident took place in March 2010, the same year he was scheduled to sign autographs at Frontier Field. The appearance was canceled. Desperate to save himself, he became a patient on VH1's reality show *Celebrity Rehab with Dr. Drew Pinsky* in 2011. Gooden says he has been clean and sober for more than two years. Last week, he took part in Major League Baseball's celebrity softball game at Citi Field, the Mets' five-year-old ball park.

He has long been compared to close friend and former teammate Darryl Strawberry, another Mets phenom whose road to Cooperstown was derailed by drugs and other off-field issues.

"I completely understand the comparison," says Gooden, who has seven children with his two ex-wives. "Darryl and I have talked about it. Our whole lives are identical — on the field and off. Rookies of the year. Same rehab. But most importantly, he's a pastor now, getting ready to build some rehab centers. And I'm speaking at colleges, high schools and jails."

He is finding fulfillment at last.

"Baseball was always my goal, but now I have a different calling," he says. "And it's more rewarding now, helping others with their lives. It's great therapy for myself."

JENN SUHR:
ALL THAT GLITTERS IS GOLD

Published January 28, 2011

More than two years after the former Jenn Stuczynski won a silver medal at the 2008 Olympics—when her coach and future husband was roundly criticized for his reaction to her performance—she opened up about past controversies, new roles and new goals.

MUCH HAS CHANGED IN JENN STUCZYNSKI'S LIFE SINCE SHE WON a silver medal in pole vaulting at the 2008 Summer Olympic Games. For one thing, she's no longer Jenn Stuczynski. The graduate of Roberts Wesleyan College outside of Rochester married her coach, Rick Suhr, in 2010 and is now Jenn Suhr. Her long, dark locks have been replaced by a blonde bob.

And Suhr is sitting on top of the world, with the top women's vault of 2010. She leaped 4.89 meters (16 feet, ½ inch) last June at the U.S. Outdoor National Championships in Des Moines, Iowa. Russian pole vaulting queen Yelena Isinbayeva had held the world's top mark for the previous five years.

"I'm happy and healthy," Suhr says.

Before she hit the big time in pole vault, the Fredonia native was quite content being a basketball star at Roberts. When she graduated, she was first all-time in scoring with 1,819 points (she's now second), fourth in rebounds, second in steals and blocks and third in assists. As a senior, she was named National Christian College Athletic Association Player of the Year. Then she met her future husband, and her whole world changed.

Suhr was a former state wrestling champion and state runner-up in pole vault at Spencerport High near Rochester. Suhr saw Stuczynski kicking a soccer ball around at Roberts in the spring of 2004. She had height (six feet), speed and athleticism. A 15-year coach with an impressive résumé of top athletes, he approached her about trying the pole vault.

39

"No way," she told him.

She had tried it as a college sophomore and "didn't like it at all."

Suhr persisted, and Stuczynski finally agreed. In February 2005, 10 months after taking up the sport, she won the U.S. Indoor Nationals in Boston. A star was born. Jenn Suhr's resume speaks volumes about her rapid ascent: nine national titles in 10 tries, including five consecutive outdoor crowns. A silver medal at the 2008 international indoor championships, and the silver Olympic medal from Beijing that same year. In the history of women's pole-vaulting, only Isinbayeva has jumped higher. And only these two rivals ever have cleared 16 feet.

"What Jenn has done is simply astounding," Rick says proudly. "Nine national championships in 10 tries? Even if she had been pole-vaulting her whole life, that's amazing."

If the Olympics put Jenn on the map, they made a name for Rick as well. But it was attention he could have done without. He was miked during Jenn's vaults, and NBC showed him acting less than enthusiastically after she secured second place behind Isinbayeva's gold — an incredible feat given her relative inexperience in the sport.

"It's the same old, same old," Suhr told her in front of the world. "You lose in takeoff at the big heights. What're you gonna do? . . . You weren't on. You know? The warm-up didn't go well . . . What're you gonna do? Didn't have the legs. Her legs are fresh. Hey, it's a silver medal."

NBC commentator Tom Hammond criticized Suhr, telling colleague Dwight Stones: "Wow, am I missing something, Dwight? Didn't she just win a silver medal, beaten only by the world record holder? Uh, where's the joy?"

More than two years later, Rick Suhr defends his actions.

"That's the way I coach," he says. "The day I change is probably the day I shouldn't be coaching anymore. The more successful you become, the more people will dislike you and criticize you. I grew up in Spencerport, going into a wrestling match where most of the people were cheering against you. I could handle the criticism."

Jenn found it much harder to handle. She would visit online track sites and read nasty comments from people ("anonymous

Jenn Suhr was able to clear 15.7 feet, the same height she won her Olympic gold medal, during a 2003 sanctioned pole vault event on the second hole at White Birch Golf Course in Lyndonville, N.Y. Photographer: Jamie Germano

cowards hiding behind keyboards," Rick called them) ripping her outspoken coach.

"I was like, 'I can't believe they're saying this,'" Jenn says. "'They must hate me. And they must hate him.'"

Rick decided some changes were in order. The coach and athlete had been coy about their relationship for years, never admitting to anything more than a close bond. But on December 19, 2009, Rick asked Jenn to be his wife. He had received permission from her father — "I'm a traditional guy," he says — and popped the question at Crescent Beach Restaurant in Greece. Seated across from the happy couple were Jenn's parents, Mark and Sue.

"He got down on one knee and did it the traditional way," Jenn says. "And in front of my parents! Brave man!"

It was a big day for one other reason, too.

"What's funny is, it was his birthday," Jenn says, "but I was reading the wrong calendar. I went all day without mentioning his birthday until he proposed and said, 'It's my birthday.'"

Jenn had cut her hair the day before. The new look proved a good luck charm.

"I always joke that if I'd known he was going to propose, I would have cut it sooner," she says.

"That was a good haircut," Rick adds. "When you get asked to marry the next day, that's a good haircut."

Two weeks later, on January 3, 2010, the couple married at a church in Spencerport before a small group.

"We had 10 people from each side," Rick says. "We didn't want cameras. No flash bulbs, no autographs, no video."

Just one big ring. Jenn doesn't know how many carats and says she doesn't care. But it's an impressive diamond, and it gets a lot of attention.

"Even people I don't know will stop me and admire it," she says. "I love it."

Two weeks later, Jenn announced her nuptials and name change at a Millrose Games news conference in New York. Rick asked his new wife to make a few other changes that he felt would make them both stronger.

"The first thing I said after we were married is, 'I want to quit the Internet and I want to quit cell phones for a year,'" he says. "Jenn threw her cell phone in the garbage. We only had one cell phone between us, and still do. We cut the cable right out of our house. No reality TV."

Rick's reasoning was simple.

"It was time to get back to basics and prioritize: God, our families. It was like cleansing your mind."

Jenn stopped visiting Internet chat rooms and made a discovery.

"If you don't read that stuff, you don't know what's being said," she says.

The couple lives in Riga, outside of Rochester, in a 2,500-square-foot house built by Suhr in 1997. Out back is a 3,600-square-foot Quonset hut (also constructed by Suhr) where Jenn trains.

They also own a lake house in Kendall, 25 miles north of their home.

Jenn says marriage has "changed our dynamic." She explains, "It makes your priorities a little different. Pole vault is just a small part of life. Marriage is forever."

It hasn't changed their competitive nature.

"We compete a lot when we play Yahtzee at home," Rick says. "I'm winning in that . . . "

Rick has two sons who live in the area and attend Caledonia-Mumford High School. Kodiak, 18, plays basketball. Madison, 15, was the quarterback for a Red Raiders team that reached the Class D state final. Rick and Jenn laugh when asked if any little Suhrs are in the future.

"We'll leave that in God's hands," Rick says, "and see what He has in store for us."

Jenn, who is sponsored by Adidas, is healthier than she has been in three years. Last year, a nagging Achilles injury limited her to just three meets, yet she was able to be the world's best.

"It was frustrating," she admits. "But that's behind me."

Rick was energized by Jenn's top world mark for 2010.

"Isinbayeva had held that spot for so long," he says. "It'll be interesting to see how that affects her. There's a crack in the armor now."

London is calling, with the 2012 Summer Olympics on the horizon. But first, Jenn Suhr must get there. And then, perhaps, she'll be able to topple Isinbayeva, the greatest female pole-vaulter in history.

"Winning a gold would be awesome," Jenn says.

She keeps her silver medal at home.

"There's room for another one," she adds with a laugh.

2

ADVERSE CONDITIONS

My favorite stories have always been those about young people who rise to success despite numerous obstacles. Some are physical, some mental, and some are out of the athlete's control. But all of these people have been inspirational.

SKIP FLANAGAN:
HE SEES THE CHEERS

Published May 4, 2014

I was a Skip Flanagan fan two minutes into meeting him. Born deaf, he was now a standout baseball player and student at Rochester Institute of Technology, and he was eternally optimistic. When I told him at least he couldn't hear boos, he laughed. When I told him sadly that he couldn't hear cheers, he had a quick reply: "I can see them."

SKIP FLANAGAN WAS 17 MONTHS OLD WHEN DOCTORS DIAGNOSED him as deaf. His panic-stricken parents bought every book they could find on sign language, desperately hoping to connect with their son. And then one day . . .

"We were sitting with him in his high chair rolling a ball across the table," his father, Sean, recounts. "He would catch it and giggle. We would point to the ball and sign 'ball,' which is putting your fingers together several times." This went on and on. Sean and Sue Flanagan then hatched a plan.

"When he wanted the ball back, we wouldn't roll it until he signed 'ball' to us," Sean says. "He hesitated, then signed 'ball.' And we rolled it back to him with tears in our eyes."

It was truly a sign of the times — and love at first sign. Skip was playing baseball almost as soon as he was walking.

"I loved it," he says through Rochester Institute of Technology interpreter Meredith Ray. "I didn't think of it as a challenge. I just thought of it as fun."

He became not just a fan, but also a history buff.

"His favorite player is Ted Williams," his dad says. "And his room is dedicated to Ted, almost like a stalker."

Skip is still playing these days, as the junior first baseman, cleanup hitter and sunshine spreader for Rochester Institute of Technology. The 6-foot, 200-pound left-hander is still inspiring, and not just because his batting average is around .300.

"He lights up any room he's in," Tigers coach Rob Grow says. "If you walk into a room, you're drawn to certain people. You're drawn to Skip. He's the best kid I've ever been around, attitude-wise."

"We keep charts on the tendencies of hitters," University of Rochester senior infielder Nate Mulberg says. "But Skip is a hard hitter to scout, because he hits the ball everywhere. He's such a great hitter and one of the most respected players in the Liberty League."

Because he can't hear, Flanagan must look back at the home-plate umpire to see if a ball or strike was called on each pitch. An interpreter is present at all games — RIT pitcher Brian Sheridan is hard of hearing — but Flanagan communicates with his teammates through reading lips, gesturing and mouthing words to each other.

"Hearing is definitely important," RIT third baseman Walt Roman says, "but he's done a great job. He's basically out there on his own. Pop-ups, being on base . . . he has to use his vision."

Roman says he has watched Flanagan improve every year.

"He's a great ballplayer with a tremendous work ethic," Roman says. "He came here his freshman year and wasn't that big. But he had a desire to get better. He came back his sophomore year and blew it out of the water. You could tell he worked his butt off in the offseason."

He was born Sean Patrick Flanagan on December 8, 1992, in Chicago. His middle name is in honor of his brother, Patrick Flanagan, who lived only one day. The family moved to Trumbull, Connecticut, when Skip was 2 — his dad is a sales manager for the Bayer Corporation (think aspirin), and was transferred. They soon settled in Framingham, Massachusetts, about 20 miles west of Boston, so that Skip could attend the Learning Center for Deaf. He was there from ages 3 to 11, went to a public middle school for grades 6 through 8, and then was the only deaf student for four years at Bishop Feehan High School in Attleboro, Massachusetts, where he had an interpreter.

Skip's deep faith drew him to a Catholic school, and he made his mark there. He started an American Sign Language club and was a major reason the school added it to their curriculum.

Skip's deafness was traced to a recessive gene, as both his parents have cousins who are deaf. He has never used it as an excuse — "never played the deaf card," his dad says. Instead, he finds it to be an advantage in baseball.

"You can ignore all the trash talk that goes on, all the negative," says the diehard Boston Red Sox fan, who attends several games at Fenway Park each summer. "You can stay in the zone and play your game."

But what about never being able to hear cheers?

"I can see them," he says.

At a young age, a cousin who was deaf suggested that Skip read everything he could get his hands on — especially comic books.

"For one thing, they have pictures," Sean explains. "And they have slang words, like 'whatcha doin'.' You don't get that in a normal education."

Skip has devoured thousands of comic books in his 21 years. His favorites feature superheroes like Batman, The Avengers and Superman.

When Skip was 5, he wanted to play Little League in Framingham. But league officials balked.

"That wouldn't be a good idea," one man told Sean. "We wouldn't know how to handle that."

So Sean and Sue tried the town of Marlborough, 10 miles northwest of Framingham. Officials there did know how to "handle" it.

"No problem," the Flanagans were told. Sean coached the team, which included five other deaf players.

Skip played two varsity seasons at Bishop Feehan and was named to the 2011 All-Scholastic baseball team by both the *Boston Globe* and *Boston Herald*. In 2012, he became the first deaf player to compete in the annual Oldtimer Baseball Game in Cambridge, Massachusetts. The game features college-age players from the New England area wearing flannel uniforms of legendary teams like the Brooklyn Dodgers, St. Louis Browns and New York Giants. Forty players who participated in the charity game have gone on to reach the major leagues.

Peter Frates, a former Boston College captain, made a symbolic one-pitch start at first base just six months after being diagnosed

with amyotrophic lateral sclerosis, otherwise known as Lou Gehrig's
disease. Frates was wearing a No. 9 Ted Williams jersey when he was
introduced, but Boston Red Sox general manager Ben Cherington
presented him with a No. 3 Jimmie Foxx jersey (Frates had worn No.
3 throughout his career). Cherington then handed Williams' No. 9
jersey to Flanagan. Inspired by his idol, Flanagan banged out three
hits and was named Most Valuable Player.

"It was an amazing day," he says.

He started 31 of 33 games his freshman year, and hit .247 as a
pitcher-outfielder (he was 2-5 with a 10.15 earned run average on the
mound). Last year, he moved to first base, started all 39 games, and
hit .353 while leading the Tigers with 35 runs batted in. He set a sin-
gle-season RIT record with 150 at-bats.

His parents are in daily contact, whether through Skype,
texting or email. Sean's job gives him travel flexibility, and Sue is a
"volunteer extreme," her husband says, so they are at almost all of
Skip's games.

"It's 376 miles and takes five hours, 45 minutes if you don't stop,"
Sean says with a laugh.

Skip is a psychology major with a solid 3.1 grade-point average. The National Technical Institute for the Deaf at RIT provides
interpreters or note-takers for Skip and other deaf or hard-of-hearing
students.

He still has one baseball season left at RIT and plans to be at the
college for two more years, establishing a minor. He dreams of playing pro baseball, but if that doesn't work out, he would like to run a
baseball complex.

Flanagan says he wants to break "every record at RIT" before his
career ends next spring.

Well, every record but one. Roman has been hit by a pitch a
whopping 68 times, the sixth-most in Division III history.

"I don't want that one," Flanagan says, laughing. "That's a painful record."

Deaf players at the major league level are rare, but hardly
unprecedented. The most accomplished was William "Dummy" Hoy,
a center fielder from 1888 to 1902. Hoy finished with a .288 batting

average, 2,044 hits and 596 stolen bases. He is widely credited with having been the driving force behind the establishment of signals for safe and out calls, which is documented in the 2008 award-winning film *Signs of the Time* produced by Crystal Pix, a company in suburban Rochester.

In 1889, Hoy set a big-league record (since tied) by throwing out three runners at home plate in one game. The catcher who recorded all three outs was Connie Mack, who went on to become the legendary owner and manager of the Philadelphia Athletics.

"He should be in the Hall of Fame for what he contributed," says Skip, who has read extensively about Hoy.

The most recent deaf major-league player is Curtis Pride, an outfielder for six major league teams (including the 2003 Yankees). He hit .250 with 20 home runs and 82 runs batted in over 11 seasons.

Pride is now the head baseball coach at Gallaudet University, a school for the deaf and hard of hearing in Washington, D.C. He says there "weren't really any disadvantages" to being a deaf player.

"The only thing that my teammates and coaches had to make an adjustment (on) was to make sure they face me when talking to me since I read lips," Pride wrote in an email. "As far as on the field, another adjustment we made was anytime I call for the ball in the outfield, it's my ball all the way. If I feel that the other fielder is in a better position to catch the ball then I won't say anything and the fielder would just wave me off."

Pride said he was never made to feel different by other players.

"Everyone, including the fans, was very supportive," he says.

Pride recruited Flanagan and was sorry to lose out to RIT.

"He's a solid player and, more importantly, a great kid with a good head on his shoulders," Pride said. "He would have made a big impact on my program."

He has already made a big impact at RIT.

The statistics say that RIT's cleanup hitter has yet to hit a home run in college. But stats can be deceiving. Those who know him say Skip Flanagan has cleared the bases — and every hurdle — in his way.

"I just want to be judged on what I can do," he says. "Not what I can't do."

JAKE SIMMONS: GRATEFUL FOR THE GAME

Published February 17, 2013

Buffalo State basketball star Jake Simmons overcame endless adversity to become his school's all-time leading scorer. This story won a New York State Associated Press award for best sports feature, beating out the New York Times, and also won first place in the New York News Publishers Association contest. I found Jake to be remarkably poised and optimistic, given his incredible past.

HE HAD LOST SO MUCH. HIS FATHER TO PRISON. HIS MOTHER TO a vicious disease. His house to a fire. And his dignity to a man who preyed on him regularly. But Jake Simmons couldn't lose basketball.

"Basketball was my vice," he says. "It was the only thing that kept me sane. It was the only environment I could control."

So when a car accident left him paralyzed for 10 days, Simmons fought back. And when the NCAA ruled him ineligible for his senior season at Buffalo State, he fought again. He's still scoring, passing, dribbling, winning and smiling. Because basketball isn't simply Jake Simmons' life, it saved his life. The 6-foot senior guard recently broke the 41-year-old school scoring record at Buffalo State set by former National Basketball Association star Randy Smith. Along the way, he has collected numerous honors: State University of New York Athletic Conference Rookie of the Year. All-SUNYAC. All-East Region.

"I'm grateful for every minute of it," he says.

To understand where Simmons is now, you must trace the amazing path that led to this destination.

Simmons was born and raised in Rochester, New York. His mother had five children. Jake was the oldest, and the only one with a different father. His own dad had six children, of which Jake also was the oldest. His parents never married, and his dad — Jake

Simmons Sr. — was in prison for much of Jake's early life.

"He went to prison (for robbery) when I was 2, and I saw him for the first time when I was 15," Jake says. "How I met my father was amazing. No one should ever meet their parent this way."

Jake was a freshman at School of the Arts and was playing basketball with friends one day when a van pulled up and a man got out. The man, just out of prison, had been driving around with his sister-in-law when he saw the boys playing. He wanted to watch and couldn't stop staring at Jake.

"I said, 'Man, that kid can play," Jake Sr. recounts. "'plays like me. He even *looks* like me!'"

The man approached the group and asked if one of them was Jake Simmons Jr.

"I am," Jake said.

The man showed Jake a photo of him as a toddler, and they embraced.

"You're my dad," Jake said to the man in wonderment.

"Yup," the man said. "I'm your dad."

The shock of meeting his real dad took an emotional toll on Jake.

"Most nights would end with me in tears," he says, "because I didn't know how to deal with it."

Gradually, father and son bonded. Today, they remain very close.

"He's actually a really good guy and I talk to him all the time," Simmons says of Jake Sr., now married and working as a personal care aide. "He's very supportive and comes to a lot of my games."

His relationship with his stepfather was far more complicated and included countless episodes of mental and physical abuse, Jake says.

"He would call me ugly," he says. "He would buy his kids candy and cupcakes and make me watch them eat. One time, he made me run outside in my bare feet and I stepped on a rusty nail. Another time, I didn't laugh at one of his jokes. He was a janitor with a huge set of keys. He threw the keys at me so hard one of them stuck in my arm, and I started bleeding. I still have the scar."

The stepfather now is in prison, convicted of raping a child. Jake never told his mother about the abuse.

"She was so sick at the time, and my telling her would have only made things worse," he says.

Kris Matthews, Jake's mom, suffered from sarcoidosis, a disease characterized by inflammation of tissues in the body. It's prevalent among young black women.

"It breaks down your immune system and organs," Jake says. "When my mom was first diagnosed, they told her she had the worst case in the United States."

She visited specialists in Florida and Ohio, but the disease intensified.

"The only medicine they could give her was a steroid called prednisone," Jake says, "and that made her heavy."

Kris Matthews succumbed to the disease in 2005, six years after being diagnosed. She was only 35. Jake was 19. Although Jake could do nothing to stop the disease from ravaging his mother, he did save her life once. In April 2003, the family home on Oakman Street burned down after a television cord caught on fire in a bedroom. Jake was playing basketball across the street.

"I saw smoke coming from the chimney," he says. "We had a fireplace so I thought it was a regular fire."

When one of his friends told him the house was on fire, Jake ran across the street and found his mother lying down.

"The smoke detectors were going off, and the house was filled with smoke," Jake recalls. "She told me to save myself, but I grabbed her and pulled her out. We were both choking."

Many people called Jake a hero, but he didn't see it that way.

"This is my mother," he says. "I would do anything to save her."

Kris Matthews is buried in Riverside Cemetery off Lake Avenue in Rochester. Jake visits twice a year religiously.

"I go on Mother's Day and on November 1," he says. "That was her birthday."

After the house fire, the Red Cross set Jake's mom and her kids up in an extended stay hotel and gave them a $500 stipend. That didn't go far for a large family, and Jake says each child wore one outfit to school every day for three months.

"Same socks, same sneakers," he says. "I didn't get a haircut. I

Buffalo State's Jake Simmons drives against Brockport's John Ivy during a 2013 game played at Brockport. Photographer: Adrian Kraus

took three buses to get to school. I was determined to go to school because that's all I had."

Some classmates mocked him for wearing the same clothes.

"Those words didn't hurt, they motivated me," he says. "I knew if education was as important as everyone said it was, that would be my way of getting out of that situation."

The family lived in a hotel for six months while a house was built for them on the west side of the city.

"My mom had broken her hip getting out of the house during the fire," Simmons says. "The meds made her heavier than her bone structure could support. So we needed a house in the city that was handicapped accessible."

Tomas Vazquez-Simmons is Jake's half brother from the same father. The two didn't meet until they were teenagers but became close friends through their love of sports. Vazquez-Simmons, who went on to play pro basketball in Puerto Rico, marvels at Jake's resilience.

"A lot of people in the same situation, it would be over for them," he says. "Basketball has been his driving force, a way for him to escape from reality. It's allowed him to get through a lot of bad things in his life."

Baseball was Simmons' first love. The slick-fielding shortstop didn't play competitive basketball until he was 13.

"My cousin asked me one day to join his church league," he says. "He took me to the gym and I started shooting. I didn't know basketball was going to play an integral role in my life. I just knew it felt good to play."

He played three varsity seasons at School of the Arts, winning a Section V championship his sophomore year and averaging 17 points as a senior. College seemed the next step, but his mother's deteriorating condition put that on hold.

"After my mom died, I was devastated," he says. "Mom was such a big part of me playing basketball. With her passing, it became too much."

For the first time in his life, basketball couldn't take away the pain.

Simmons spent three years after high school working, mainly as a manager for a cell phone store. He would hang with friends on street corners but says he resisted drugs.

"Why make a bad situation worse?" he says.

His friends urged him to return to school, saying, "You don't belong here. You're different from us."

Finally, in the fall of 2007, Simmons enrolled at Finger Lakes Community College near Canandaigua, New York. He planned to resume his basketball career but never got the chance. On October 15, 2007, Simmons was driving to school when a woman driving a Lincoln Town Car swerved into him and sent his small car spinning out of control. It flipped over a guardrail and landed in the opposite expressway. Jake suffered a broken left ankle and bruised back, plus a cut on his head.

"I went home for a couple of days, but then I woke up one morning and couldn't feel my legs. I realized I was paralyzed."

He went to the hospital, where doctors performed one test after another, trying to figure out what was wrong. Then, mysteriously and without diagnosis, he could walk again.

"They never did find out what was wrong," he says.

He wasn't actually scouted by Buffalo State coach Fajri Ansari. The coach ran an Amateur Athletic Union team and was watching Vazquez-Simmons when a friend mentioned that Vazquez-Simmons had an older brother who had been through a lot and was a pretty good player.

"I've worked in admissions for years, and my first thought was that I'd like to help this kid," Ansari says. "Then I went to a summer league to see him and I said, 'Shoot, this kid can play.'"

Simmons has shined since he stepped foot on campus, averaging 16.8 points his freshman year and improving on that every season.

"He's the best shooter I've ever coached," Ansari says. "But he doesn't take it for granted. He works on shooting."

On December 14, Simmons woke up with a tingling sensation in his fingers and just knew.

"I called my dad and said, 'I'm going to break the school record tonight,'" he recalls.

His father was skeptical.

"You need 33 points," he said.

"Come to the game," Jake told him.

Simmons did not score 33 points against Central Penn that night. He scored a career-high 43 and beat a 41-year-old school record set by Smith, the 1978 NBA All-Star Game Most Valuable Player.

"I didn't even know who Randy Smith was before I got here," Simmons says. "And then that's all I saw: 'Randy Smith. Randy Smith.' It's such an honor."

Smith's mark of 1,712, compiled over three seasons (freshmen weren't allowed to play on varsity back then), had stood since 1971. And if it hadn't been for the persistence of Simmons and Ansari, the record would still be Smith's. Because in the summer of 2012, the NCAA ruled that Simmons had played his last college game, stating that his "athletic" clock had begun when he entered FLCC and had expired the previous spring. He also had briefly been enrolled at Monroe Community College in Rochester before coming to Buffalo State. Simmons badgered doctors, high school teachers, even a chiropractor for notes that would help his cause. "I spent the whole summer working on this," he says "And when they finally said 'yes' (last fall), it was a like a weight had been lifted off my shoulders."

Simmons switched his major from theatre tech to individualized studies and expects to graduate next fall. He hopes to play ball overseas, but his dream job is to travel the country as a motivational speaker. He already has spoken at Buffalo State, a few Rochester-area high schools (including School of the Arts' graduation ceremony last June) and some detention centers in Buffalo.

His message is simple.

"If you feel the world doesn't get any better from here, it does," he says. "I thought that once. It gets better with time. The higher your education is, the more you can set goals and open up doors. Don't stop. Because if you stop, you limit your potential."

His dad can't stop gushing about his oldest son, his resilient son.

"I'm so proud of that boy," Jake Sr. says. "He's got that strong spirit, that determination and will to do better. He volunteers at (local) youth basketball camps and all the kids look up to him.

I always told him, 'Jake, don't be like me. Be better than me.'"

Jake Jr. smiles when asked what his mom would think of him now.

"I know she'd be proud of me," he says. "I was never a bad kid and I went to her for all kinds of advice: girls, anything. She'd be so proud that I took her advice and used it for nothing but positive in my life. And I became a man."

JOE VICARIO: THE PROUDEST TIGER

Published October 20, 2013

Joe Vicario underwent 31 surgeries in his first 21 years, backed by a family that literally went bankrupt twice to save him. Unable to play the game he loves, he became student manager of the Division I Rochester Institute of Technology hockey teams.

NOTHING GETS JOE VICARIO DOWN. NOT THE 28 SURGERIES HE endured in his first 12 years. Not the two cancer surgeries or emergency abdominal surgery last winter. Not the syndrome that left him with a heart defect and without two organs, a thumb, and an ear.

"I don't think negative," the Buffalo native says. "My mom always taught me to be positive. I don't let anything get me down."

Vicario has never skated a minute for the RIT Tigers, but the junior is a huge cog in the daily operation of the men's and women's Division I hockey programs. The student manager is the one who coordinates the pregame meal, hangs the uniforms, cleans the locker room and carries the coolers. And he's the one with the remarkable story of perseverance. Year after year, surgery after surgery, challenge after challenge.

Vicario was born five weeks premature on January 2, 1992, in Buffalo, New York, and doctors weren't sure if he or his mother would live. Martha Vicario had experienced a placental abruption — where the placenta separates from the uterus before the baby is born. An emergency Caesarean section took place, and Joe entered the world at 4 pounds, 10 ounces. Martha had torn her placenta at 11 weeks and began going once a week for sonograms.

"All the doctors knew then was that Joe was missing his left kidney," Martha Vicario says. "But they said there are millions of people with one kidney."

But he was also born with a number of other issues: No left ear, left lung or left thumb. His aortic heart valve is bicuspid instead of

61

*Joe Vicario, student manager for the RIT men's hockey team, right, on the
bench before the Tigers' 2013 home opener against Colgate at Ritter Arena.
Photographer: Jamie Germano*

the normal tricuspid, something that happens in less than two percent of the population. He still has regular checkups for that. All of
the vertebrae on his left side are fused with his neck, meaning he
could never play contact sports. His left arm is shorter than his right.
Doctors diagnosed him with Goldenhar syndrome, a rare congenital defect characterized by incomplete development of the ear, nose,
palate and lip, abnormalities in the formation of the face and head
and underdeveloped or absent organs.

"It was unbelievable," Martha says of hearing the news. "It was
devastating."

Martha and her husband Chuck took their boy home and raised
him as normally as possible while he endured one surgery after
another. Four on his hand (doctors rotated his left index finger to
give him a thumb). Three so that he could use his left arm. One for
his kidney (urine was blackflowing into the organ). Another for a
hernia. And so on.

"It has been very hard for the entire family: emotionally, physically and financially," his mom says.

Even though doctors told them they had only a two percent chance of having another child with Goldenhar, Martha and Chuck waited 10 anxious years to expand their family. Jeremy was born in 2002 and Julia followed two years later.

"They look up to me," Joe says proudly. "I love them so much."

Martha is a stay-at-home mom. Chuck is a machine operator at a Goodyear Dunlop Tires plant. Each time Martha gave birth, Chuck was laid off, and Joe's medical bills kept piling up. Martha says the bed in the intensive care nursery was $80,000. The recent rounds of unexpected surgeries cost $67,000 (medical insurance has defrayed some of the cost), and the total since Joe's birth is more than $1 million. Chuck and Martha have had to file for bankruptcy twice just to keep their home.

"That's why Joey has worked so hard," Martha says. "He has told me many times, 'Mom, no matter what I'm going to get a good job so you and Dad don't have to worry, because you've sacrificed everything for me, Jeremy and Julia.'"

Through it all, Joe never lost his sweet disposition. When he was in second grade, he learned that a girl in kindergarten was scared of him because of his looks. Joe asked the school principal if he could speak to the girl, and the principal agreed.

"I don't want you to be scared of me," he told the girl. "This is the way God made me."

His parents fought hard to give him a proper education. One psychologist diagnosed him as being severely mentally retarded in elementary school. Martha and Chuck didn't believe it, and it took five years before they found the perfect place for him at St. Mary's School for the Deaf in downtown Buffalo.

"Joe went from getting 50s and 60s to being on the honor roll," his mother says proudly. "We were told he'd never learn sign language because he couldn't use his left arm. He learned sign language in six weeks."

Vicario loved sports, especially going to Buffalo Sabres games. His dad had been a member of the Junior Sabres, and Joe dreamed of following in his skates. But he knew that was impossible. Instead, he got involved in sports as student manager of the St. Mary's soccer, basketball and track teams. He embraced it and became so popular that he received 20 academic and athletic awards by the time he graduated in 2010. Yes, athletic awards. Joe Vicario, who never kicked a ball, shot a jumper or ran a yard, was named St. Mary's Student-Athlete of the Year as a senior. His mother put all 20 plaques on the walls of his room back home, and there they remain.

"How proud am I?" she asks. And then she begins to weep. "I'm very proud. Joey is my inspiration."

Although he says he wasn't bullied, Joe did face his share of ostracism from peers. But he didn't buckle. He didn't flinch.

"My mom set me on the right path," he says. "She told me to always be strong, tough, positive. I owe so much to my parents, I really do."

The 5-foot-7 Vicario has been at Rochester Institute of Technology for three years but has endured three leaves of absence. The first leave came his freshman year, when stomach pains and stress made college overwhelming. The second took place last fall, when he was diagnosed with cancer. The third came earlier this year, when he underwent emergency surgery. He was already accepted at RIT when he saw the 2010 men's hockey team's run to the Frozen Four on national TV.

"I thought it was just great," he says. "And I have always loved hockey, so I wanted to be a part of the team."

He emailed Wilson, who passed it on to Jeff Siegel, RIT's director of hockey operations. Siegel had been a student manager in college and found a lot of similarities between Vicario's email and the one he had once sent to a hockey coach.

"We met, and it was clear right away that I wanted Joe to be part of us," Siegel says. "I babied him at first, because I didn't know what he could do. But he was carrying heavier coolers than me."

Vicario was a volunteer the first two years and now receives minimum wage. And it is clearly Joe's show.

"He won't even let me touch the jerseys," Siegel says with a laugh. "He talks to them. He's very superstitious."

And a bit obsessed with cleanliness. If Vicario spies even one speck of lint on the floor of the RIT locker room, he pounces on it.

"I can't stand anything on the tiger (logo on the center of the carpet)," he says.

One Saturday in 2013, the Tigers left campus for an afternoon practice at Blue Cross Arena in downtown Rochester before their game against national power Michigan. Associate head coach Brian Hills and assistant Dave Insalaco were showing recruits around Ritter Arena, the Tigers' former on-campus rink, when they saw Vicario.

"What are you doing here?" Hills asked. "Why aren't you with the team?"

"I have to take care of the meals for the boys when they come back," Vicario answered. "I want to make sure it's taken care of."

Hills laughs at the memory.

"That's Joe," he says. "He'll do anything for the team, and everyone loves him. Who wouldn't love him? He's a total part of the team."

Wilson says Vicario always shows up with a smile and a positive attitude.

"It's just amazing considering everything he has gone through," the 15th-year coach says. "He's just a great kid."

Wilson nicknamed him "Part-Time Joe" because the team never knows when Vicario will be around. He majors in applied computer technology at RIT's National Technical Institute for the Deaf and a full slate of classes limits his attendance at practice. He rarely goes on the road with the team.

"He's here and then he isn't," Wilson says. "Part-Time Joe."

Vicario loved the name so much he put it on his Facebook profile.

"PTJ, that's me," he says with a smile.

On November 23, 2012, the day after Thanksgiving, Vicario was diagnosed with stage 1B testicular cancer.

"I thought I was done with surgeries," he says. "But I wasn't."

Vicario took a medical leave from RIT and underwent his first surgery on November 30, 2012 and his second on January 7, 2013 — just five days after his 21st birthday. Chemotherapy was not a true option because of his medical condition. As a precaution, Vicario's doctor removed his lymph nodes under the intestines up to where his left kidney would be. His left testicle and surrounding tissue also were removed. He has been cancer free for nine months but must undergo regular CT scans and have blood work done every three months for the next five years.

The RIT players decided to surprise him on his 21st birthday. Seven of them plus Siegel showed up at Vicario's home in Amherst with a white stretch limo. They took Joe, his parents, his siblings and his grandmother to the Seneca Niagara Casino for an evening of gambling, dinner and laughs. The Vicarios spent the night at the hotel in a suite.

"And I even won $200 playing roulette," Joe says with a laugh. "It was awesome. I consider the team my family. I love those guys."

The feeling is mutual.

"Joe is an inspiration to all of us," junior forward and team captain Matt Garbowsky says. "He puts everything in perspective."

He's not going away anytime soon. Vicario has more than a year left at RIT before he graduates, which means he'll be around when the new Gene Polisseni Center opens for hockey next fall.

"We joke that he's stalling just to be in the new arena," Siegel says, "but the truth is we all love having him around."

Two months after his surprise party, Vicario was back in the hospital. He had experienced stomach pain on and off for three years, almost always after eating, and doctors had passed it off as acid reflux. But on March 12, the pain was agonizing and Vicario became ill in his bathroom. He called his mom, who notified Siegel. He called 911, and Joe was taken by ambulance to Strong Memorial Hospital as his parents raced from Amherst to Rochester.

Doctors discovered a complete mess when they opened Vicario up.

"Everything was free floating," his mother says. "His stomach, colon, spleen, intestines . . . they found his spleen near his liver on the right side. It's supposed to be on the left."

Joe had been missing important connective tissue, something his parents never knew until that night. His esophagus was twisted and his stomach was stuck up in his chest cavity by his heart.

While doctors were operating, they removed his appendix as

a preventive measure. He spent two weeks in the hospital before returning to school — and his beloved job as hockey student manager. Vicario was visited in the hospital by several Tigers plus Wilson, and Hills, who was on crutches following hip surgery.

"The little stuff I was going through was nothing compared to what he's going through," Hills says. "Joe is an inspiration to us. He battles back from everything."

Despite this back-to-back whammy — cancer and emergency surgery — Vicario manages to light a candle where others curse the darkness.

"If I'd had the chemo for my cancer, I wouldn't have been able to have the stomach surgery," he says. "I would have died within 24 hours. It was a blessing."

Vicario loves watching ESPN and reality shows like *Big Brother* and *Survivor*. He's addicted to Dole's strawberry kiwi juice, and his favorite food is his mom's lasagna.

"But I'm full-blooded Italian, so I love all Italian food," he says.

He's a regular on Facebook and Twitter and is as eloquent as he is dedicated.

"Be good," reads one post. "If you can't be good, be great."

Another: "If you're going through hell, keep going."

He has a driver's license, although he doesn't have a car. He lives alone in an on-campus dorm but is expected to gain a roommate this academic year. He has few regrets despite his numerous obstacles, but one is that he will never play the game his father played before him.

"That kind of bothers me," he says. "I wanted to follow in his path."

In many ways, he already has. Vicario knows he'll never score a goal or beat the syndrome that has been with him for 21 challenging years. He prays every day for God to keep him strong and healthy. He posts on Facebook, "I can and I will survive!"

Most of all, he's happy with who he is.

"Everything happens for a reason, and it's not a bad reason," he says. "I live the way I can. I'm here. I'm me. Life is good."

BOBBY GRECO:
A PASSION FOR THE GAME

Published October 14, 2012

Bobby Greco has loved football since he was a boy, but he was born with a rare congenital disorder that prevented him from walking. That didn't stop the Buffalo native from becoming an assistant coach for the St. John Fisher College football team—and a friend of Pro Football Hall of Famer Jim Kelly.

BOBBY GRECO'S FATHER WAS RECENTLY APPROACHED BY A friend who had seen some photos of Bobby on Facebook. There he was, coaching at Jim Kelly's football camp in Buffalo. And there he was, meeting Yankees legend Joe Torre at CitiField, home of the New York Mets.

"He's so lucky," the friend told Bobby's dad. "I'd love to be your son."

The story made Bobby laugh.

"I told my dad, 'Gladly. I would accept the trade. If he wants to come and take the pain, I'll let him take it.'"

Bobby lives with pain every day. He's confined to a wheelchair and can't move his limbs. He is averaging one surgery for every year of his life. But the boy who doctors said would never have any semblance of a life is an assistant offensive line coach for the nationally ranked St. John Fisher football team. He's also a student at Fisher.

"I don't know what ever happened to those doctors," Greco says, managing a smile. "Doctors now call me a medical mystery."

Greco — it's pronounced GREEK-o — was born June 3, 1989, and has lived his entire life in Geneva, a small city on the shores of Seneca Lake in upstate New York.

"When the doctors delivered him, we knew right away there was a problem," his dad, Bob Sr., says. "They started examining him and broke his femur."

Bobby eventually was diagnosed with arthrogryposis, a rare congenital disorder characterized by multiple joint contractures. The condition affects the proper formation of ligaments and muscles. He can move his hands only enough to drive his electric wheelchair and must be fed, dressed and showered daily. He sleeps in a recliner chair because the special bed he needs is so costly.

Most of his medical expenses are covered by Medicaid, but not everything. The van that transports him is on its last wheels. He desperately needs a shower chair, but that's $800.

"Things that will make his life a little more bearable," his dad says. "He's in pain 24/7, but he doesn't let people know. He doesn't want them to think of him in that way."

At birth, all of Greco's joints were locked and most were out of place. He underwent 21 surgeries in his first 14 years — many in his first three years. Most were orthopedic surgeries to turn the joints the correct way. Both hips, his legs, his right arm. There wasn't enough muscle in his left arm to allow for surgery. At 1, both legs and both arms were in splints. At 9, he underwent a spinal fusion.

"That was terrible," he says. "I was in the hospital for eight weeks."

Through it all, his large family formed his support system. One cousin even celebrated her birthday in Bobby's hospital room, just so he could be there. Doctors had told Bob and JoAnn Greco that their son would never show emotion, never talk, never have any quality of life. Some recommended that he be institutionalized.

"It wasn't an option," his dad says. "We told them, 'He's our son. We're taking him home.'"

Bobby fooled everyone. By 3, he was on a parapodium — which allows standing without the aid of crutches — and using a computer with the aid of a head pointer. And he showed remarkable intelligence for his age.

"We went from learning how to deal with a handicapped child to how to deal with a gifted one," his dad says proudly.

Through the pain and the endless hospital stays, Bobby found comfort in watching football with his semifamous dad. Bob Greco was the lead singer for the popular party band Nik and the Nice Guys for 18 years, and they played at Buffalo Bills Super Bowl appearances, tailgate and Christmas parties and quarterback Jim Kelly's parties.

Bobby became a huge Bills fan, watching games regularly with his dad during Buffalo's four-year Super Bowl run. In 1995, when he was 6, he got a chance to meet his heroes. Kelly had brought his StarGaze charity softball tournament, a mix of rock stars and athletes, to Rochester's Silver Stadium. Bobby met Kelly — already his idol — plus Dan Marino and Bills stars Bruce Smith, Thurman Thomas, James Lofton and Pete Metzelaars.

Bobby was in football heaven.

"Just meeting everyone that day lit a fire," he says. "I knew I wanted to do something with football."

At 6, he didn't yet realize he could never play the game.

"He used to ask me, 'Can you make me walk? I want to play football,'" his dad recalls.

Reality soon set in, but Bobby's passion for football didn't diminish.

"If I couldn't play, I wanted to coach," he says.

Bobby began going to Bills games and meeting the players. Offensive lineman Adam Lingner once let Bobby try on his American Football Conference championship ring.

"I'll earn my own as a coach someday," Bobby told him.

Bobby's coaching career began in eighth grade. His cousin, Joe Davis, was a former high school football star who also was Bobby's aide. Davis was an assistant coach on the Geneva modified team and asked if Bobby wanted to help out.

"I loved everything about it," Greco says. "The planning, the camaraderie. I tried to learn everything I could."

He spent one year on modified, one on junior varsity and three on the varsity staff. Many nights after practice, his legs would bleed from sitting in a wheelchair for 12 hours. But he wouldn't stop.

In 2006, his senior year, he was named homecoming king. But his biggest satisfaction came later that fall, when unbeaten Geneva won the Class B state championship.

Bobby graduated from Geneva with a 93 average. He knew St. John Fisher had a strong sports management program and, after touring the school, realized this was where he wanted to go. When

*St. John Fisher assistant football coach Bobby Greco watches a play during a
2012 practice. Photographer: Kris Murante*

Greco paid head football coach Paul Vosburgh a visit and offered to
help out with the linemen, Vosburgh gave the OK.

"The only thing we worried about was if he was on the sideline,
can he get out of the way if someone (on the field) runs into him,"
Vosburgh says. "But it's never happened. He keeps back with the
linemen."

Greco lived on campus and took classes at the Pittsford school
his freshman year. A wicked battle with vasculitis (inflammation of
the blood vessels) forced him to miss much of his sophomore year.

"That was a really bad year," he says.

This year, Bobby is living with his parents in Geneva and taking
Fisher courses online. He has six rotating aides who dress him,
shower him and drive him around. Most of them, like 24-year-old
Kyle Olschewske, are also longtime friends.

"Bobby perseveres through anything," Olschewske says. "He never lets anything get him down. If there's an obstacle, he'll persevere through it."

Although he has never played the game and is barely older than the players he coaches, Greco commands their respect. Zach Bassett, a junior offensive tackle, first met Greco at a summer Finger Lakes football camp in Geneva.

"I came here and Bobby remembered who I was," Bassett says. "As a freshman, you don't know the steps, but he guides us through, even though he's never done the steps himself. He's very soft-spoken, but what he has to say is very encouraging and very informational."

Vosburgh says his student assistant knows his football.

"He has a good working knowledge of the game," Vosburgh says, "and I don't know if anyone loves football as much as Bobby."

Greco stayed in touch with Kelly. More than once, the Pro Football Hall of Famer has invited Greco to be a coach at his annual summer camp and a dinner guest at his home. But the Bills legend isn't Greco's only famous friend.

"One time I walked in on him and he was on the phone talking and really happy," his dad recounts. "It was (ESPN's) Chris Berman."

Former Bills receiver Andre Reed has invited Greco to the team's alumni game. Hall of Fame quarterback Dan Marino, who also met Greco at that 1995 softball game, chats him up at Kelly's parties.

Kelly, who lost his 8-year-old son, Hunter, to a terrible disease in 2005, finds himself inspired by the young man from Geneva.

"I saw what my son went through every day," Kelly says. "God bless Bobby. He's a fighter. I wish there were more people with that drive who weren't handicapped."

Kelly is humbled that his meeting with Bobby 17 years ago inspired the young boy to follow this unlikely path.

"You never go into something to have accolades thrown your way," he says. "But it makes you feel good that you were able to help."

If this sounds like the script for a Hollywood movie, there's a reason: a screenplay is in the works, and Bobby's manager — Buffalo-based Therese Forton-Barnes — is shopping the movie rights around.

"He's a fascinating and inspiring story," she says.

Greco would love to stay in coaching after graduation, and his eye remains on that most special of prizes: head coach in the NFL (but he'll take an assistant's job too, thank you very much).

"Why not?" he asks.

There are plenty of days when Bob, now the lead singer of The Bob Greco Band, and JoAnn, a registered nurse, stare at their only child and marvel at what has transpired. The boy who was not supposed to show emotion has a wicked sense of humor and a dream that won't die.

"We used to watch him on the field at Geneva, then at Fisher and at the Ralph coaching with Jim Kelly," Bob Sr. says. "He wants a job that only 32 people have. Who am I to tell him it can't happen? He's beaten the odds over and over. He's doing it in front of our eyes."

MARK MUENCH:
A FIGHT TO THE FINISH

Published May 12, 2010

*Mark Muench was a Rochester-area businessman and an
avid sports fan who received a frightening diagnosis in 2009.
That's when his competitive nature took over.*

WHEN MARK MUENCH WAS DIAGNOSED WITH BRAIN CANCER IN
November 2009, doctors didn't exactly sugarcoat the prognosis.

"There's no cure for what you have," his oncologist said. Muench
didn't flinch. "Well doc, I'm all about firsts," he replied.

Six months later, Muench received the Christine Wagner Welch
Inspiration Award at the 61st annual Rochester Press-Radio Club
Award dinner. Of the 1,200 guests on hand, 300 were there to support him. When Muench was told he was receiving the award, his
first thought was, "There are a million people more deserving." He
would be wrong there. Since he was diagnosed, Muench has been
the picture of dignity and grace under fire.

"Mark is one of those rare people God put on the earth to
help the rest of us enjoy life a bit more," says close friend John
Doyle, who introduced Muench at the dinner. "He's been such an
inspiration."

Muench (rhymes with "bench") is a Syracuse native who graduated from St. John Fisher College in Pittsford, New York, in 1977. He
is self-employed as a manufacturer's rep and jokes that "you use my
products all the time when you go to Wegmans," a Rochester-based
supermarket giant. His company, Triple M Packaging, distributes
the bags used at stores such as Wegmans and Dick's Sporting Goods.
It's the type of job that requires a "people person," and you won't
find a better one than Muench.

"He has thousands of numbers in his iPhone," says Mary, his
wife of 32 years. "I went through his list one day, thinking they were

all business related. But they were all personal friends. He talks to a dozen guys each week from all over. He works at developing relationships."

Mark and Mary have triplet sons: Andrew, Christopher and Brian. Andrew developed encephalitis due to a tainted vaccine when he was a baby. He is partially blind, has limited speech and is in a wheelchair. He lives in a group home in Penfield and sees his family each weekend.

Mark was watching Chris and Brian play Little League baseball years ago when he discovered a Challenger game nearby. Challenger features physically and mentally challenged children. Mark signed Andrew up, became heavily involved in the organization and now is the director of Fairport Challenger.

Muench's first sign that something was wrong came on a golfing trip with friends to Kiawah Island, South Carolina, in October. He suddenly felt lightheaded, sat down briefly, and then finished the round. Similar episodes followed for the next several weeks. He went to Strong Memorial Hospital in Rochester and also visited his own physician, but he passed all the tests. On November 8, he nearly passed out at his kitchen table and was taken to the hospital, where a CAT scan showed a glioblastoma tumor. Surgery was performed to remove most of the tumor, and Muench began treatment.

He has completed three rounds of chemo and one 30-day round of radiation. His hair is beginning to grow back, and he has gained back 10 of the 20 pounds he lost, with the help of steroids. But he has lost his strength and is partially paralyzed on his right side. And part of the tumor remains.

"The goal is to shrink it or keep it the same size," Mark says.

A 7-handicap golfer and longtime member at prestigious Monroe Golf Club, he finds swinging clubs "frustrating" these days.

"I just do the best I can," he says.

Since he began his blog, he has reconnected with grammar school friends and received about 2,000 cards and emails.

But that's not all. When Wegmans officials heard about Muench's illness, they assured him that he would remain their rep and that he was "part of the Wegmans family."

Boyhood friend Peter Waters flew Mark and Brian, along with friend Mike Thornton, to Boston on Easter for the Yankees-Red Sox season opener.

Neighbor Kevin Flynn owns a plane and often flies the friendly skies with Muench.

Good friend Ed Stack, the CEO of Dick's Sporting Goods and the first person Muench met at St. John Fisher, has offered his corporate jet should the Muench family need to travel for future alternative treatments anywhere in the world.

Doyle, a Syracuse University graduate, set up a meeting between Muench and SU basketball coach Jim Boeheim. Muench came away with a handful of signed basketballs, which he plans to give to friends.

Muench has been a Syracuse University football and basketball season ticketholder for 25 years. "I bleed Orange," he says.

He's an avid photographer who will take your picture minutes after meeting you.

"He's your instant friend," Doyle says.

Mark and Mary are religious people whose faith has only deepened. They pray for a miracle and constantly notice "signs" that someone is listening.

Mark has preached from the beginning of this challenge about "faith, family and friends." He even wrote it on his blog.

Not long after, Mary was shopping at a Hallmark store when she came upon a small rectangular sign with the words "Faith, Family, Friends."

She purchased it, and thought, "This is wild."

Another "sign" came recently when they attended a seminar and were introduced to a man who asked about their primary focus. Mary told him she was interested in brain stem cell research in the Philippines. The man told them he was an expert in brain stem cell research and would like to speak with them further.

"Of all the people (to meet)," Mary says.

Then there's Bill Moore of Victor. He was diagnosed with a glioblastoma tumor — 15 years ago.

"He's my hero," Mark says. "And he works for Wegmans, my No. 1 customer. Another sign."

Muench is soft-spoken and modest, but he's also a fighter. When he met his doctors for the first time, he gave a bold prediction.

"Someday, you're going to do an MRI on me and say, 'Where did that tumor go?'" he told them.

One doctor remarked, "Well, Mark, if that happens it will be the first time that's ever happened."

"I'm all about firsts," Muench said.

POSTSCRIPT

On March 20, 2014, Mark Muench lost his battle with cancer. He lived four years and four months after his diagnosis.

PHIL AND MARIE ROOF: DEARLY DEPARTED

Published May 26, 2005

Phil Roof had just begun his third season as manager of the Triple-A Rochester Red Wings baseball team when tragedy struck: His wife, Marie, was stricken with terminal cancer. This story profiled their struggle to accept the inevitable.

AS THE BEIGE LINCOLN TOWN CAR MOTORED TOWARD ITS DESTI-nation three weeks ago, and the "Rochester" signs appeared on the highway, Tommy Klemenz grew excited in the back seat.

"Rah, rah, rah!" he yelled with a smile. "Rah, rah, rah!"

Red Wings manager Phil Roof stared straight ahead in the driver's seat, listening sadly to his brother-in-law.

"Rah, rah, rah is his translation for Rochester Red Wings," Roof explained. "He thought we were going to Rochester, New York."

Sadly, that was not the case. Phil was driving his wife, Marie, to the Mayo Clinic in Rochester, Minnesota, a 706-mile trek from their home in Boaz, Kentucky. They brought along Tommy, 43, who has Down syndrome and whose legal guardians are the Roofs. They went to fight cancer, an aggressive enemy that has struck Marie hard.

"We went there looking for answers," Phil says, "and for a way to beat this thing."

The first omen came last fall. Back home in Kentucky, after Phil's second season with the Red Wings, Marie underwent her annual physical, and her doctor noticed a high enzyme count. A month later, another test showed the count near normal.

"Our daughters had gotten on the Internet and it said this was a precursor to cancer," Phil says. "I told the doctor, 'If this is a serious matter, I'll quit my job.' He said 'No, I wouldn't do that.' So we kind of forgot about it."

In early March, Marie felt pain in her lower back and pelvic

79

area. She had accompanied Phil to Fort Myers, Florida, for spring training, and her daily 1½-mile walk had become so painful that she eventually stopped. Phil asked the Minnesota Twins doctor to look at his wife. They ruled out a ruptured disc because she still had strength in her legs and lower back. Arthritis was possible, they said.

When spring training ended April 3, Marie returned with Tommy to Kentucky and Phil headed north with the Red Wings. On April 20, Marie underwent an MRI. Phil was in Buffalo with the Wings when the call came from his beloved wife of 41 years.

"Phil, I have bad news," Marie told him. "I have cancer. It's in my lungs and lower back."

Phil didn't hesitate. "I'm coming home," he said.

He took an indefinite leave of absence from the Wings, handing over the reins to coach Rich Miller. At 64, he had planned for this to be his final season in baseball. But he had never planned on this ending.

"Sometimes you suspect the worst in life," Roof says. "In reality, that came about."

Roof headed to Rochester. Then, after an emotional meeting with members of the front office, he was driven to his apartment by general manager Dan Mason.

"You know, Mase," he said, packing his suitcase, "forty-one years feels like two weeks right now."

He was home that evening.

The Roofs are deeply religious people who believe in God's will. But they will do anything to put their world back on its axis. Phil called Terry Ryan, the Minnesota Twins general manager.

"We need a second opinion," he said. "Do you think I could get into the Mayo Clinic?"

As luck would have it, Twins owner Carl Pohlad is a major contributor to the world-famous hospital. Within 24 hours, the Roofs were making plans to head to Rochester, Minnestoa, for an evaluation. That week, they arrived and Marie was put on a treatment plan.

Earlier this month, she underwent a week of radiation concentrated on her pelvis, lower back and brain. The next week, it was strictly the brain.

"I asked the doctor, 'Why aren't we treating the tumor on the lung?'" Roof said. "He said 'Phil, we've got to clear up the tumor in the brain first. If that fails, everything else is a waste of time.'"

The radiation treatment itself lasts 15 minutes. The prep work is much more involved. A frame is made for the head, the body is strapped down and blocks are put in place to prevent any movement.

"We get in there and get out," Roof says. "An hour later, she's fatigued. She comes home and sleeps."

"Home" during their two-week stay in Minnesota was a two-bedroom condo owned by Anna Restovich, the older sister of ex-Red Wings outfielder Michael Restovich. Michael was placed on waivers by the Twins in late March, but Anna graciously gave up her condo, located five blocks from the Mayo Clinic, and moved in with her parents.

"They are an incredible family," Roof says.

On May 15, Ryan invited Roof to the Metrodome in Minneapolis to see the Twins play the Texas Rangers. He walked into the clubhouse and received more hugs and handshakes than a politician on the campaign trail. Then he sat and watched many of his former players contribute to a 5-2 Twins victory.

"I needed a day like that," he says.

Friday, the Roofs and Tommy drove back home to Kentucky. In a few weeks, Marie will undergo another MRI to see if the brain tumor has shrunk. Chemotherapy may also begin soon.

The Roofs have been overwhelmed by the support they have received — from the Twins organization, the Restoviches and numerous Red Wings fans. Phil has received more than 200 phone calls, including one from former Red Wing Jeromy Palki, who's pitching in Mexico. The Red Wings players raised $500 to help defray some of Phil and Marie's expenses, and the front office matched it.

"We've received well over 100 cards from well-wishers," Phil says. "Tommy goes out each day to put mail in the box and to bring the mail in. It's his job, and he's proud of it. You can't do it. He wants to do it."

Tommy is aware that something is wrong with his big sister but doesn't realize how serious the situation is.

When Phil and Tommy would pick Marie up after her treatment, he would hug and kiss her, shouting "Rie-rie!"

Marie has been overwhelmed by the support. She wrote a statement this week for use in this article. It read:

To the Red Wings community and fans in Rochester:
We were overwhelmed when we returned home from the Mayo Clinic in Rochester, Minnesota to find so many cards, letters and get-well wishes. Your care and concern has been an inspiration and courage for us to face this challenge in our lives. A sincere thanks for all your support.

Roof has tried to follow the Red Wings as closely as possible during his month away. He reads stories on the Internet and speaks with Miller and pitching coach Bobby Cuellar regularly.

"I'm just tickled to death that they are playing well," he says.

He spends most of his time on the Internet educating himself about cancer, as do his four daughters, who are spread out in Kentucky, Oregon, Missouri, and California.

"Everything we can get our hands on," Phil says.

Melanie lives in Lancaster, California, with her husband Chris, a rocket scientist at Edwards Air Force Base. Melanie gave birth to Phil and Marie's seventh grandchild in May 2005, a boy named Carson Christopher Sturgis.

The Roofs say Marie's illness has deepened their faith.

"We can't get over the number of people praying for her recovery," Roof says. "The rosary is part of our everyday life. It's never entered our minds to ask 'Why us?'"

The Roofs are involved with nine different doctors. Four are in Kentucky and four are in Minnesota. The other, Dr. Kenneth Pennington of Indiana, is the father-in-law of Red Wings outfielder Todd Dunwoody.

"He's the one we throw questions on the wall to, and he gives us his undivided opinion," Roof says.

Marie's prognosis is not good.

"I asked the radiation doctor, 'Are you treating this for recovery or remission?'" Phil says. "He said, 'Remission.' He said the survival rate is less than a year."

Phil has noticed "more quietness" about Marie.

"She's always been outgoing, the life of the family," he says. "Now she's quiet and reserved."

Marie is a longtime smoker. Her mother and sister died of cancer. "I have to think it's in the genes," Phil says.

He is asked the question everyone asks: Will you return as Red Wings manager?

"It doesn't look good," he says. "We've got to do everything we can to educate ourselves. What scares me is it's in the fourth stage, and it's in several areas."

Phil remembers last fall, when he was mulling retirement, how Marie urged him to give it one more year.

"If she said no, I would have stopped right there," he says. "She's my wife, my best friend, my confidante."

The fight continues as the cards pour in.

"As a doctor told me, 'Miracles do happen,'" Phil says. "That's what we are focusing on. Miracles do happen."

Despite their constant prayers, Marie Roof passed away at a nursing home in Paducah, Kentucky on December 11, 2005, after an eight-month battle with cancer. She was 63.

"We were married 15,023 days," said Phil, who was at her side when she died.

Phil never did return to the Red Wings, although for several years he has helped the Twins at their spring training camp in Fort Myers, Florida. Eventually, he found another reason to live and love.

In the summer of 2006, Roof was introduced to Linda Sanger, his cousin's best friend for 60 years, at a wedding reception in Hickman, Kentucky. They talked. They clicked. Phil asked if he could call her again, and she said yes.

"We had lunch that Wednesday, and we've been doing great ever since," Phil says.

He proposed in November. She said yes again. And they married the following February, six days before Phil reported to Twins camp.

Dan Mason had driven Roof to the Rochester airport the day the manager found out Marie had cancer.

"It was one of the toughest situations I've ever encountered as
GM," Mason says. "Phil is one of the kindest people you'll ever meet
in your life. He's usually extremely upbeat and optimistic, but he
was having a horrible time with this."

The day after Thanksgiving, Mason received an email from Roof
with "Wedding in the planning" in the subject line.

"He's always sending me stuff, and I figured this was a joke,"
Mason says.

It was no joke.

"Dan, I'm going to marry that lady I met in July," Roof wrote.

Although Mason was surprised by the news, he was happy for
his friend.

"Nobody knows what Phil went through, having to care for
Marie and Tommy," he says. "He told me, 'Dan, I'm lonely. I wish I
had someone to talk to.'

"Phil deserves to be happy."

Roof had Marie's approval.

"She told me before she died that I had her blessing to marry
again," Phil says. "She even picked a woman out for me."

Then he laughs.

"But I'm not going to mention her name now."

Laughing is something this gentle man did very little of in the
weeks and months following Marie's death. Lost without her, Phil
joined a grieving group that met twice a month.

One day, he noticed a sad, 76-year-old man who had been widowed for four years.

"He was down and out," Roof says. "I told my daughter, 'Darla, I
will not allow grieving to take hold of me like that.'"

His cousin, Lucy Strong, had regularly visited the Roofs during
Marie's illness, and she continued coming to bring Phil coffeecake
and company after Marie died. One day in May, she mentioned that
her best friend had moved to Paducah and had been widowed for
10 years.

"She'd be a good companion for you in this grieving process,"
Lucy told him. "Whenever you're ready to meet her, I'll introduce you."

Roof didn't pursue the matter at first.

"My group suggested that you get out and socialize," he says. "They didn't say to date. It didn't cross my mind."

Weeks later, Phil and Linda met at the wedding reception, and he was impressed by her love and knowledge of sports.

"That's what the connection is all about," Roof says. "She's a big UK (University of Kentucky) fan, both football and basketball. Her two daughters went there."

She's learning about baseball, too. Roof took her to a St. Louis Cardinals-Pittsburgh Pirates game in St. Louis in September.

"She'd only been to one big league game in her lifetime before that," he says. "She's learning."

Roof's four grown daughters weren't thrilled about the impending marriage at first.

"They were a little concerned about it being too quick," Roof says. "I told them, 'I'll be 66 in March. I don't want to wait a long time. I found someone I love and want to marry.'"

Tommy also seems OK with it. He was extremely close to Marie, who was more like a mother than an older sister, but he calls Sanger "Lin" and seems happy for Phil.

The couple will live in Sanger's house after the wedding.

"I wouldn't ask her to come live in my house with all of Marie's possessions there," Roof says.

Tommy also has moved on. His twin, Greg Klemenz, recently called Phil and offered to have Tommy live with him and his wife, Mindy, in Louisville.

"Greg said it's time for the Klemenzes to step forward," Roof says. "I assured him and Mindy I'd stay in touch on a daily basis."

Like an old Beatles song, Roof's life has changed in oh so many ways. He cherishes the memory of Marie but is looking forward to this new, uncharted chapter in his life.

"This all happened by accident," he says. "I'm a very lucky guy."

POSTSCRIPT

Tommy Klemenz passed away on September 19, 2009 at age 48. He is buried near his sister, Marie, in Paducah, Kentucky.

JEANETTE GLOVER: FULL HOUSE

Published February 21, 1997

Canada native Jeanette Glover went from one foster home to another growing up. She became a basketball star at Roberts Wesleyan College, and a hero to her extended—and we mean extended—foster family back home.

JEANETTE GLOVER HAD A WAY OF DEALING WITH THE CURVE LIFE had thrown her while she shuffled from foster home to foster home. She would stand under the rim and throw her basketball through the bottom of the net, hoping it swished through on the way down.

"It was fun for me," she said. "I wanted to score twice."

Knowing the ball would come down was about the only certainty in Glover's life. By 9, she had been in more than a dozen foster homes and lost track of her natural parents. Her grades suffered and she saw less of her four brothers. Then Wendy and Frank Glover changed everything. They adopted Jeanette and her siblings into their suburban Toronto home in 1985. Then they adopted more. And more. And more. Jeanette now is one of 16 adopted children ranging in age from 3 to 20. The Glovers also raised two older biological children. There are five girls and 13 boys in all.

Jeanette also has found a home at Roberts Wesleyan College, outside of Rochester, New York. The 5-foot-10 freshman forward leads the Raiders with 17.8 points and 11.5 rebounds per game, and her 61.2 percent field goal percentage ranks third in the National Association of Intercollegiate Athletics. By comparison, National Basketball Association leader Tyrone Hill of Cleveland shoots 59.1 percent.

Glover always seems to have a smile on her face — no surprise considering where she was, and where she is now.

Jeanette struggles to remember her biological parents, saying, "I think their names are John and Joanne." She was born in Calgary, Canada, to an African father and a Guyanese mother in 1976. When brother Jason came along a year later, the father took the young children to his native Nigeria.

"His goal was to eventually bring everyone back with him," Glover said. "He left us with his mother when he went back to Calgary, but his mother died and we were taken care of by several relatives."

By the time Glover returned to Calgary at age 4, brother Charles had been born. Jeffrey came along three years later and Jonathan the year after that.

"My parents kept splitting up and getting back together," Glover said. "And every time they did, another baby came along."

The marriage continued to founder, and the children remained for a short time with their mother, whom Jeanette described as a manic depressive who beat them. Children's Aid Care eventually sent the children to different foster homes.

"We'd live with one family for a while, then go back to our mother," Jeanette recalled. "She had several chances to take us back, but she couldn't do it because of her financial situation."

Jeanette said her father disappeared from her life when she was 5. The children continued to split time between foster homes and their mother's care, sometimes not seeing each other for two months. This continued until Jeanette was 9. One day, her mother left the kids with a relative and vanished.

"It was a big thing," Jeanette said. "The police came and everyone searched through the neighborhood. A family took us in for a while, and they were rich, but they couldn't keep us for good."

Police learned the mother had disappeared into the United States. The children haven't seen her since.

Frank Glover's mother was scanning through the *Toronto Star* one day in 1985 when an unusual ad caught her eye.

An article called "Today's Child," featuring children who were difficult to place, detailed the plight of Jeanette and her four brothers, who ranged in age from 2 to 8.

Frank and Wendy were raising their children, Danielle and James, and had hoped for more. But Wendy was stricken with ovarian cancer in 1974, and it seemed like the big family they had longed for would never develop.

A phone call from Frank's mother changed that. She told the Glovers about the ad.

The biggest strike against the Glovers was their race.

"They try to place children with people of the same culture," Wendy said.

It took eight months, but eventually the Glovers adopted all five children. Three more were adopted 18 months later, and over the next 11 years the Glovers continued adding children in need of parents.

Now, Sweet 16 has a whole different meaning for the Glovers.

"We love them as if they were our own blood," Wendy says.

In all, there are five families in one, with Jeanette the oldest of the adopted kids.

That's the way they became the Glover bunch.

Frank Glover, 46, owns and manages an automobile leasing company in Toronto. His large family lives in a three-story mansion in Scarborough, a few miles from downtown Toronto.

It is a home fit for a football team — or a family of 20. There are 13 bedrooms and five bathrooms, with a living room on each floor. The home also has a pool, a jungle gym and a concrete basketball court, where children from all over come to play.

"I'll look out and see 13 kids playing," Wendy Glover said, "and they're not my kids!"

In the winter, the Glovers freeze the court and play hockey.

Wendy used to work as a supervisor in a day-care center. In a way, she still does. She cleans the house and cooks and manages a weekly grocery bill of $700.

The children play, and fight, and play again. Like any family.

"There is constant activity. The house is alive from morning until night," Wendy says.

This is not a home without its problems. Six of the children were addicted to drugs when they were born and still need special care. Jeanette has become a hero in the household. "She's a great role model," Wendy says. "The children love her. They know she's top dog."

You'll find Jeanette diving for loose balls in practice and games, jumping for rebounds as if her life depended on the outcome, sometimes forgetting to play defense in her zeal to touch the ball.

"I need to touch it all the time," says Glover, who moved into the starting lineup last month.

Glover is a superior athlete who is still learning how to play. She set a school record at People's Christian School in Toronto as a senior, scoring 51 points in a game.

"I didn't know terms like 'post up' or 'pick and roll,'" she said. "We never played man-to-man, and I always used just my right hand.

I've learned a lot here, and I'm still learning."

Says Roberts coach Mike Faro: "She's a real raw talent. Some things she does extremely well. Other things she needs work on, like defense."

Glover improved herself off the court, too. Her grades used to hover in the 60s but moved into the high 80s after she received helped from a tutor in high school. Glover discovered Roberts Wesleyan when she saw a school pamphlet at a college fair. This fall, her grade point average was 3.0. Glover doesn't complain. She remembers where she was.

"I remember earlier this season we came home after a loss," Faro says. "She didn't say anything the whole way home."

The team dispersed after arriving at Roberts, and it was near midnight when Faro walked outside to drive his assistant home.

That was when he saw Glover.

"She was running around the track," Faro says. "It was the middle of winter and she was running a few miles outside. She probably didn't feel she did the job she should have. That's how she dealt with it."

ERIN MUIR: SOCCER MOM

Published November 8, 2002

*Erin Muir nearly lost her family and her future after
becoming pregnant at 16. But then a strange thing happened:
the birth of her daughter brought the family back together,
and Muir went on to play Division I soccer.*

THIS IS A STORY ABOUT LIFE AND DEATH. ABOUT A HOUSE DIVIDED, and then rebuilt. It's about anger and pain, forgiveness and renewal. But mostly, it's the story of a little girl who has changed a lot of lives.

Erin Muir had big plans. Scouted by Olympic development soccer officials as a teenager, the forward/midfielder from Spencerport — a town west of Rochester, New York — hoped to land an athletic scholarship to a Division I college. Her dream came true this fall when she began playing for the University of Massachusetts, but the ride from Spencerport to Amherst took longer than the usual five hours. This one took four years and was anything but smooth. In that time, Muir became pregnant at 16 and a mom at 17. She turned down major colleges, fought relentlessly with her parents, ended her relationship with the baby's father and gave up soccer to complete her associate's degree.

She landed the full ride to UMass after one of the program's star players was killed last June in a one-car accident.

"It's been a lot," Muir says.

A lot of highs and lows. But always, in her deepest moments of despair, there has been McKennzie . . . that smiling girl with the big brown eyes.

By her junior year at Spencerport High, in 1997, Muir's goal of playing Division I soccer seemed imminent. She set a school record with 18 goals and enjoyed one fabulous game against Churchville-Chili in which she scored four goals and assisted on four more. She was a member of the Olympic Development Program and the

Empire State Games scholastic team and was active in track and skiing. Several Division I colleges had contacted her.

"Erin was on the radar screen for ODP as a freshman," her father, Larry, says. "She was on the fast track."

That track was derailed during Muir's junior year. She met a man named Shawn at a local gym and the two immediately hit it off. She was 16. He was 23. Eventually, the relationship became intimate.

"She thought she was in love," says her mother, Linda.

Erin was 4½ months pregnant when she learned she was expecting.

"I was suspicious," she says, "but I had gone on and off skipping periods previously."

When Muir began getting nauseated while training for ODP, she visited her doctor. That's when she learned she was pregnant.

"I think I got sick and just cried," she says. "There was a feeling of panic, but also of getting information and figuring out what I could do."

First, she had to tell her parents.

"They are well-infiltrated [sic] through the town and the soccer community," she says. "It was not easy. It took them a very long time to be OK with it."

The relationship between Erin and her parents became strained.

"It ran the circle of emotions," Larry says. "There was anger and hurt. It threw the house into a tizzy. We had shared goals, and this put a real wrench in the works."

The Muirs received incredible support from their friends, but it didn't dull the pain.

"People who had been through something similar would say, 'It will be better in time,'" Linda says. "At the time, I was grieving so much that I didn't want to hear it. It was like, 'Don't tell me I'm going to be happy.'"

A month before she found out she was pregnant, Erin had competed in an ODP tournament in Florida over Christmas break. She was scheduled to play in Germany that April.

"I had just mailed a check toward the next event and came home all excited," her dad says. "When she told us, that happiness came to a screeching halt."

Muir's parents suggested that Erin put the baby up for adoption, and all the plans were soon in place.

"We actually had a family picked out and everything," Erin says.

But all bets were off when McKennzie Lynne was born on June 29, 1998.

"I knew in the back of my head I wasn't going to put her up," says Muir, 21. "I just wanted my parents to know I was looking at every option.

"It was really sad the whole time in the hospital. I didn't want to give her up for adoption because I felt I'd regret it for a very long time. But I was afraid that if I kept her my parents would disown me."

Finally, she says, "It came down to what I felt was right."

The family agreed on one thing: McKennzie was something to behold.

"Our love for the baby was immediate," Larry says. "There was no doubt about that."

Adds Erin: "I fell in love with her right away."

Erin says she received support from her friends.

"Nowadays I think it happens to so many people but you don't hear about it because of abortions," she says. "I think people were shocked, but I got a lot of respect for going to school and keeping the baby."

Muir returned to Spencerport for her senior year and played soccer that fall. She agreed to play at West Virginia University, and then decided she couldn't make such a long move with an infant daughter. Instead, she played two years at Monroe Community College and helped lead the Tribunes to consecutive national junior-college championship appearances, earning All-America honors her second year.

"She played everywhere," Monroe Community College coach Tracey Britton says. "We put her wherever we needed her that day and she was able to help us."

Britton says Muir's best role was as a mother.

"It was amazing to watch Erin," she says. "She's a very good mom."

After her sophomore year, several Division I schools pursued Muir, but she was reluctant to commit to playing away from home.

"All these coaches are telling me, 'Don't you understand the opportunity you have?'" Muir told Britton one day. "Don't they understand? It's not about me anymore. It's about McKennzie."

Muir spent last year working as a receptionist at a local hair salon while completing her associate's degree.

"I thought she was done playing soccer," her mom says.

But Muir's dream of playing at Division I remained.

Last summer, she began talking with Syracuse University women's soccer coach April Kater about joining the Orangewomen. But Kater was able to offer only a partial scholarship, and Muir didn't have enough tuition money. It appeared Division I would have to wait again.

Early last June, UMass soccer star Stephanie Santos was killed in a one-car accident in Granby, Massachusetts. Santos had been the leading scorer on the Massachusetts women's team as a freshman the previous fall. She was the passenger in a car driven by a former high school teammate. The tragedy sent shock waves throughout the tight-knit UMass soccer community. Kater, a three-time soccer All-American at UMass, drove up to give her condolences to head coach Jim Rudy. While talking, Kater mentioned Muir's name to her former coach and said she felt Muir would be a good addition.

"Being the incredibly loyal UMass grad that she is, she let us know even though we were going to be opponents this year," Rudy says.

In July, Muir accepted a full scholarship to UMass.

McKennzie stays at her dad's house during the week, talking by phone to her mom almost nightly.

On the weekends, the Muirs take McKennzie to see Erin.

These weekends in New England run the gamut of emotions.

"It's so awesome when I see her," says Erin, who lives in a family housing apartment. "And it's so sad when she leaves."

McKennzie is an energetic, happy girl who loves Disney movies (*Little Mermaid 2* is her favorite) and playing soccer.

"She's already playing with 8-year-olds," her mom says. "She's so excited when she's playing. She could run forever."

The relationship with Shawn is over, but the responsibility of raising McKennzie is something both parents have embraced.

"Shawn is a good father," Muir says. "He is doing a lot to help me have this opportunity."

The wounds between Erin's parents and Shawn also have healed.

"He has been so wonderful," Linda Muir says. "He's so great about making sure McKennzie gets to preschool. He's really stepped up to the plate."

Erin is doing what she always wanted: Playing Division I soccer and gaining a college education.

The junior is a psychology major with a minor in biology. She hopes one day to work in pharmaceutical sales or as an elementary school psychologist.

"I feel that as I accomplish more of the goals I had, and my parents had for me, things continue to get better between us," she says.

She credits her family and Shawn's family for helping to give her the chance to do this.

"I am beyond fortunate," she says. "A year ago, I would have never thought this was possible."

Muir started 16 games for UMass, which finished 6-11. She logged more minutes than all but three teammates.

"I thought we had a good year considering she was one year rusty and she was making the jump from junior college to a top-level Division I team," Rudy says. "And we played her out of position to capitalize on her leadership skills and organization."

Muir is no longer the scoring machine she was at Spencerport and MCC. This fall, the defender managed just one shot on goal.

That's fine. One shot is all she ever needed.

McKennzie has become quite popular with the UMass players and coaches. During a recent road trip from Pittsburgh to Olean, the little girl rode the bus with her mom and the rest of the team.

Her laughter filled the air and gave a lift to a team still reeling from the loss of their teammate.

"It's fun having McKennzie around," Rudy says, "and it's been sort of therapeutic as well. You lose someone who's older that you love and care for, and then — in a small way — we get McKennzie in return, full of life and innocence."

It's something that no victory could do for UMass.

"All those things that we lost when Stephanie died," Rudy says, "we got them back with McKennzie."

KRISTINE PIERCE:
BODY CHECKING CANCER

Published February 26, 1999

*Rochester Institute of Technology women's hockey player
Kristine Pierce was given a dire diagnosis, but forged on
against her ultimate opponent: cancer.*

KRISTINE PIERCE SAT IN HER DOCTOR'S OFFICE ON DECEMBER 2,
1996, and tried to figure out what had caused the pea-sized lump on
her neck.

"I thought maybe it was just a cyst," she recalls. "I felt awesome. I
didn't think it was a big deal."

It was.

Moments later, Pierce's doctor delivered the bad news: The
Rochester Institute of Technology freshman had Hodgkin's dis-
ease. Pierce was in denial, mumbling that she didn't know what
Hodgkin's was and she had a class at 4 p.m., anyway.

"You have cancer," the doctor told her, "and all I can tell you
is that in a year, your life will be forever changed. You will look at
everything differently."

It took six months of chemotherapy and 21 consecutive days
of radiation, but Pierce has put cancer in the penalty box. The disease caused her to miss her freshman hockey season at Rochester
Institute of Technology, yet she went on to become an All-America
defenseman. But it was Pierce's efforts off the ice that allowed her
to make history as the first female to win the prestigious Hockey
Humanitarian Award, given to "college hockey's finest citizen" at any
level, male or female. She beat out four other finalists in a ceremony
at the 1999 NCAA Division I men's Final Four in Anaheim, California.

Pierce has been involved in 27 community projects or charity
events since her freshman year at RIT, and earned 13 scholarships.
The senior has worked in a local soup kitchen, been part of the Big

Brothers/Big Sisters program, read to children in area libraries and even helped launch a Girl Scout cookie campaign. And since her illness, she has counseled others who are battling cancer.

"She's always been the type of girl that can't walk away," says her mother, Mary Ann. "When she gets involved in something that affects her life, she'll do whatever it takes to make it better for others."

Pierce has a learning disability, and in high school she participated in the "Can I Make It?" program. She was so grateful to those who advised her, that in college she began speaking at area high schools to others with similar disabilities. Pierce's battle with cancer has intensified her instincts to help others. "She doesn't waste any day," her mother says. "She makes the best out of everything, and no day is a bad day."

That's something she couldn't always say. Four years ago, Pierce had to deal with another illness that scared her more than the Hodgkin's that would follow. Her father, Larry, was suffering from a rare liver disease and needed a transplant.

"I remember I had a game here on my birthday and we went down to the Ritz [the RIT campus cafeteria]," Kristine recalls. "Dad was sitting in the corner with his beepers, looking all jaundiced-colored. I remember looking at him and making my wish as I was cutting the cake: 'Please give him a transplant.'"

Two days later, Larry Pierce got the phone call he had been waiting for and received his new liver.

"It was the scariest time of my life," Kristine says. "When something is happening to you, you can control it. When the doctor said I had Hodgkin's, I was like, 'OK, what do we have to do?' It was just another hurdle to overcome."

Pierce's positive attitude has helped her become a strong hockey player as well. She spent most of her teenage years playing in the Rochester Youth Hockey League on boys' teams, but was such a natural leader that her teammates named her a captain when she was 13.

Her high school, Honeoye Falls-Lima, doesn't have a varsity hockey team, so she skated with a McQuaid Jesuit squad that included her younger brother, Larry Jr., now a defenseman at Cornell University.

"She impressed me right away," says Al Vyverberg, McQuaid's hockey coach for 14 seasons until becoming an assistant this year. "She doesn't sit around; she goes and gets things done. When you hear about this (hockey humanitarian) award, you go, 'Holy moly, that's her!'"

Pierce says she was "on top of the world" when she entered RIT in 1996. She loved college life and, for the first time, she could play on a women's hockey team for her school.

"I felt invincible," she says.

But two days before Thanksgiving, she discovered that lump on the left side of her neck. Her parents insisted she have it examined.

A week later, she was given the somber news at Highland Hospital. Although she was in denial, there was something very real about the effect the chemo treatments were having on her. She gained 65 pounds, her hair became paper thin, and it was a chore just to walk. Her low point came on her 21st birthday. She was alone at her parents' home when a gift basket arrived from family friends in Florida.

"I started going through it and suddenly it hit me: 'God, what if I'm not here next year?'" she says. "I got really sad."

Her doctor gave her the best prescription for recovery, telling her, "Do you want to live or die? Attitude is everything, Kristine."

Pierce learned she was clear of the disease on August 8, 1997.

"I look at things completely different now," she says. "I don't take anything for granted, and the simplest things in life are the best."

Pierce always loved to volunteer her time, but after her bout with cancer, she took on more roles, even serving on a committee to renovate the cancer center at Strong Hospital.

And she willingly talked with cancer patients about what to expect, and about how "attitude is everything."

"I'd volunteer my whole life if I could," she says. "My dad would hate it, because I wouldn't get paid, but I'd do it."

"She always has her hand in something," her father says. "She gets that from her mother, who is a tremendous person."

The Hockey Humanitarian Award is big, second in stature only to the Hobey Baker Award that goes to college hockey's top player.

There are hundreds of players at divisions I, II and III, but Pierce stood out among the others. John Greenhalgh is the founding director of the award, and when he received her nomination from RIT sports information director Chuck Mitrano, he laughed out loud.

"She's not eligible," Greenhalgh kidded Mitrano. "She's an angel."

BOB WARD:
THE (HEART) BEAT GOES ON

Published November 9, 1999

St. John Fisher basketball coach Bob Ward was given a second chance at life
after suffering a heart attack while driving to Oneonta, New York, to watch a
football game. Fortunately, he lived two minutes from the hospital.

JON BOON NEARLY ASKED TO SEE BOB WARD'S DRIVER'S LICENSE
Sunday during St. John Fisher College's basketball scrimmage with
Clarkson. He couldn't believe this was the same intense coach who
was once thrown out of a game with his team ahead by six points.

"I kept waiting for him to lose his temper," says Boon, Fisher's
sixth-year assistant. "I even lost a bet with his wife. It took Bob 35 minutes to say anything to an official. I thought it would only take five."

Ward has a reason for his transformation from Mr. Hyde into Mr.
Rogers. Basketball is no longer life or death to him.

Ward faced death six weeks ago "and cheated it," he says.

This is one opponent he plans to keep down.

September 24, 1999, was shaping up like any other Friday during
Ward's life, which meant he would be away from his home in Canandaigua, a picturesque city of around 10,000 on Canandaigua Lake.

"I'll bet you I haven't stayed home on a Friday in 20 years," he
said from his office at Fisher, where he serves as both head men's
basketball coach and athletic director. "I'm either at practice, or
recruiting, or going on the road. In the summer, I'm at camp or on
the golf course."

But Ward's 14-year-old daughter, Morghan, had undergone
knee surgery the week before and was still recuperating. Ward's
wife, Kimberly, had spent several days caring for Morghan, and
Bob decided this would be his turn — at least until 3 p.m., when
he would drive to Oneonta to watch Fisher's football team play
Hartwick. But at 2:45, Ward began having serious chest pains.

He took some Tums, and then called his wife when the pain didn't subside.

Against his better judgment, Ward got in the car. "But by then," he says, "I was sweating and really in pain." Fortunately, he lives only two minutes from F.F. Thompson Hospital and decided to check into the emergency room — a minor miracle in itself.

"I'm the type of person who would rather take 25 Tums than go to the hospital," he says. "But you reach a point where the pain is so great it's telling you one thing: 'This is a heart attack.'"

Ward was placed on a hospital bed, and doctors began performing routine tests on him. Suddenly, he saw a "shimmering, bright light" before passing out.

"They tell me I was out for only about a minute," he says. "When I woke up, there were 8 to 10 people all over me. I knew something was wrong."

Ward's heart had stopped, and doctors had to use paddles from the defibrillator to shock it into beating again. Kim later told her husband his skin color had changed to gray, then yellow.

"There's no doubt I'm a lucky man," Ward says. "If I'm on the road, I'm dead."

Three days later, he was transferred to Rochester General Hospital, where doctors discovered 90 percent blockage in one artery and 70 percent in another. An angiogram was performed, Ward's arteries were unclogged, and he was sent home soon after. He was told to stay away from the rigors of coaching for six weeks, and he obeyed doctor's orders.

"They showed me photos of my arteries before and after," he says. "It was like the difference between driving on a back road and being on 490."

Ward is 53 and looks 45. He felt 20, which was part of the problem.

"I'm around all these young people all the time and I think of myself as being younger," says Ward, whose father died of a heart attack at 69. "You don't realize that you're getting older."

Ward didn't drink or smoke, and he worked out on the Stair-Master about four times a week. But his eating habits were terrible.

"Because I'm around young players, my diet was too much like a

22-year-old," he says. "Chicken wings, burgers, pizza . . . and eating at buffets late at night."

Ward felt chest pains 18 months ago after a road game, but the pain disappeared and he thought nothing of it.

"Now (doctors) are telling me that was a heart attack," he says.

He also felt burning sensations many times after working out but passed them off as indigestion.

"That's a warning sign I missed," he says.

Ward stands 6-1 and weighed 219 before his heart attack. Since then, he has dropped 20 pounds and says he feels "20 years younger."

"My clothes feel better and I don't have that sluggish feeling," he says. "I have more energy now than I did before the attack."

He eats oat cereal for breakfast, and chicken, fish and salad for lunch and dinner. He hasn't touched soda — diet or sugar — since his attack.

Ward did not escape without some harm: A small part of his left ventricle was damaged. But because doctors were able to care for him promptly, the impact was minimal. Doctors have told him he could easily live another 30 years, and he doesn't plan to let them down. That may lead to his stepping down as coach, perhaps as early as next season.

"I need time to evaluate my life and the coaching part of it," says Ward, who regularly puts in 80- or 90-hour work weeks during the season with his administrative duties, his coaching and recruiting.

Ward is one of the area's most successful coaches. His teams annually make the NCAA Division III Tournament, and he has recorded an impressive 226-90 record at Fisher since taking over the program from Bobby Wanzer, a former star for the Rochester Royals of the National Basketball Association from 1947-57.

Nobody runs the gamut of emotions — anguish, joy, frustration — like Ward, but he promises to tone it down.

"I admit I have an 'A' type personality," he says. "I'm high-strung, and that's probably not good for the work I do. But I'm certainly not going to kill myself doing this job."

He promises a kinder, gentler Bob Ward when the season begins. Boon isn't sure that will happen.

"I don't think Bob is going to change at 53," he says. "Look at guys like (NFL coaches) Dan Reeves and Mike Ditka. They both had heart problems, and they're still intense. But I'll give Bob credit. He listened to his doctors and stayed away for six weeks. That had to be very hard on him."

Perhaps not as hard as one might expect.

"This has been almost a spiritual experience," Ward says. "Nobody wants to think about their mortality, but I believe I was very lucky.

"God bless little Morghan!"

CHARLOTTE REARDON: BREATHING LESSONS

Published September 24, 2003

I rarely interview "average" athletes, but I was more than willing to make an exception for University of Rochester runner Charlotte Reardon. Not only did she suffer from asthma, but she also was battling cystic fibrosis. A courageous young woman with a great story.

AS A TEENAGER GROWING UP IN OLNEY, MARYLAND, CHARLOTTE Reardon loved sports. But sports didn't love her back.

"I went out for field hockey and soccer and got cut," she says. "I wanted to be a cheerleader so bad, but I tried out twice and got cut."

Basketball? No way.

"I have a height deficiency," says the 5-foot-5 Reardon. "And I'm terrible."

She eventually turned to running.

"I couldn't get cut from the track team," she explains, "because there were no cuts."

At first Reardon was so slow that her 100-meter time could have been clocked with a calendar. But she gradually improved, and now she's a freshman on the University of Rochester cross-country team.

It would be a nice story of persistence and resilience for anyone else, but it's a tale of determination, defiance and pure courage for Reardon.

She was born with cystic fibrosis, a genetic disorder that affects the respiratory, digestive and reproductive systems. A disease that kills.

"With my limited knowledge, I just figured she wouldn't be able to run," says UR coach Barbara Hartwig. "I never would have imagined it."

Reardon is no threat to make the NCAA Division III Championships, but with a personal-best time of 20 minutes, 50 seconds for 5 kilometers, she is hardly embarrassing herself.

"She's middle of the team," Hartwig says, "but she's such a positive force for us. Even as a freshman, it's obvious she's going to have an impact on this team, whether it's by running or by leadership. I think it's going to be both."

Reardon didn't suffer CF's full effects until third grade.

"I was always aware I had it," she says. "My parents never hid it from me."

As her condition worsened, Reardon's father would provide regular treatments. John Reardon would cup his hands and pat his daughter on the back to loosen the mucus in her lungs and unblock her airways. By third grade, she was making yearly hospital visits to receive antibiotics and therapy four times a day. By seventh grade, the hospital visits had become twice a year.

That was when doctors inserted a gastrointestinal tube in her stomach. A pump was hooked up to the tube, and predigested food with extra calories was filtered into her system.

"They had to do it, because I was so short and scrawny," she says. "I was so little growing up that I'd get infections in my lungs and they would build on each other."

There was one positive to the experience.

"You don't taste the food," she says. "That's good because it's disgusting."

Reardon is now a healthy 5-foot-5, 120 pounds and hasn't used the pump in a long time.

Her first experiences with running came when she was a youngster growing up in Olney, 20 miles outside of Washington, D.C.

"Dad made me run," she says. "I hated it so much I would cry. But it helped me with CF."

After failing at several sports, she went out for track with a few other friends in the spring of her sophomore year at Good Counsel High School.

"I didn't even get a jersey," she says. "The coach wasn't mean. He just said, 'You're not going to race on varsity, and we need the jersey.'"

Undaunted, Reardon went out for cross-country the following fall — and promptly suffered three stress fractures in her legs.

"I don't absorb nutrients like everyone else," explains Reardon, who didn't finish a race that fall of her junior year.

But she stayed with it, worked out with a friend all winter and competed on the varsity track team that spring.

"That really did it for me," she says. "I became hardcore and ran all summer. I wasn't the best by any means, but I was competitive."

Reardon became Good Counsel's inspirational leader, handing out Gatorade bottles she had adorned with messages and wrapped in ribbon.

"Everyone is scared before a race, and I have a book of quotes for running, so I would give them to my teammates," she says. "I'm such a nerd."

Reardon's coach, Tom Arnold, told a Washington Post reporter about her, and the media soon began flocking to practices and meets: ESPN even featured her on SportsCenter.

"It got a little annoying," says Reardon, who was featured in an advertising segment in a recent issue of Sports Illustrated.

"I said, 'Coach, I don't get it.' And he said, 'Charlotte, if it helps even one person, it's worth it.'"

Reardon realized that when she received a letter from a young woman in Maryland.

"She said she had just given birth to a baby with CF and she had read about me," Reardon says. "She said, 'Now I know that my son is not doomed.'"

Reardon finished second at Good Counsel's conference meet, helping the school to a second-place finish. When she visited UR last summer, two members of the Yellowjackets' cross-country team showed her around.

"They were so nice and it was such a beautiful campus, I knew I wanted to come here," she says.

She runs 35 to 40 miles per week.

"I find it actually helps me with my lungs," says Reardon, who also suffers from asthma. "I enjoy it."

"Most people don't know about CF," she says. "Horrible things can happen. If I catch the common cold, I could wind up in the hospital because my immune system is much lower than (that of) the average person."

And, she says, "You can die."

Reardon loves to dance, although she is the first to admit she has two left feet.

"I'm a spaz," she says.

She also enjoys country music and rap, loves ham and shrimp and watches *Will & Grace*, although she hasn't watched TV since she arrived on campus.

Reardon's major is undeclared, but she hopes to work in a science field. She plans to continue running after learning a valuable lesson this past summer.

"I took it easy and didn't run much," she says, "and I wound up in the hospital. I need to run. It helps me."

Reardon wants to coach cross-country and track someday.

She also would like to marry eventually and have children. She knows there is a 50 percent chance that her baby would have CF if the father is not a carrier and a 75 percent chance if he is.

"I'm not worried about it," she says. "I have CF. If someone is going to have kids with CF, who better than me?"

Reardon hasn't finished higher than 25th in any race this fall and may never win a college event.

No matter. She has a bigger opponent to battle, and every time she crosses the finish line she feels like a champion.

3

BEHIND THE SCENES

One of my favorite "genres" is to be the proverbial fly on the wall and tell readers what is going on behind the scenes. I've done that on several occasions throughout the years, hanging for hours with an athlete or team and taking meticulous notes so that I can bring it all back to life. Here are a few of my favorite stories.

MURPH SHAPIRO: EARNING HIS STRIPES

Published February 21, 1999

*On a cold winter's night in 1999, I got in the car with Bruce "Murph"
Shapiro, then the athletic director at Monroe Community College in
Rochester, New York, and wrote a referee's account of the
St. Bonaventure-Rhode Island Division I men's basketball game
in Olean, New York, about two hours south of Rochester.*

MADISON SQUARE GARDEN, 1981. TOP-RANKED NORTH CAROLINA
is playing Rutgers, and referee Murph Shapiro is in awe.

"I'm like 'Holy smokes, Dean Smith!' he recalls. "I had never
reffed a game that he was coaching before. I'd never even met him."

Shapiro waits to shake Smith's hand before the game, but the
North Carolina coaching legend doesn't leave his spot on the bench.

"Gee, that's odd," Shapiro thinks.

Two plays into the game, the ball accidentally glances off a
Rutgers player's leg in front of the Carolina bench. Smith is furious.

"Murph, that was a kick!" he bellows at the ref. "Murph!"

"I'm thinking, 'How does he know my name?'" Shapiro says.
"'How does he know my name?' But he knew."

5:42 p.m. Shapiro is dressed in a tan sports coat, with blue pants
and tie, as he drives out of the Monroe Community College campus.

"We are about to pick up a lieutenant-colonel in the United
States Army," he says, beaming. "He also happens to be a great
basketball official."

Officer Ken Clark is waiting in the lobby of the Thruway
Marriott and gets into the back seat when the car pulls up. The desti-
nation is Olean, New York.

By day, Shapiro is athletic director at MCC and Clark works
at the Pentagon in Washington, D.C. In four hours, both will be on

center stage as officials in a nationally televised Atlantic 10 basketball game between Rhode Island and St. Bonaventure.

"I hope we don't have to make a lot of calls," Shapiro says. "I hope the ball goes in the basket all night, because when it does, wonderful things happen. No rebounds, no guys climbing on top of each other. And the ball isn't rolling on the floor with guys diving after it."

At 5-foot-7, Shapiro would have a hard time convincing anyone of his impressive basketball past. The 1957 Franklin High graduate averaged 20 points his senior season and earned a full ride to Division I Miami of Florida, where he played in the National Collegiate Athletic Association Tournament his sophomore year and the National Invitation Tournament his junior year.

"We actually turned down an NCAA bid to play in the NIT," he says. "The coach let us vote and we picked the NIT. And you know why? Because they gave watches."

Shapiro went on to coach at Monroe and Eastridge high schools before becoming MCC's first basketball coach in 1969, a position he held until 1985. Shapiro began officiating freshman and junior varsity games in the 1960s before moving up to varsity. In the mid-70s, he started working college games in the East.

"At the time, there were no leagues," he says. "Everything was under the umbrella of the ECAC, and there wasn't much traveling going on. You'd ref at Niagara, Canisius and Syracuse."

Times change. In the past 15 years, Shapiro has earned his referee's stripes in 10 NCAA Tournaments, and worked in famed arenas such as the Philadelphia Palestra (his favorite) and the "Dean Dome" in Chapel Hill, N.C.

Not to mention a few trips to Hawaii along the way.

"Do you believe in heaven?" Shapiro asks as the car glides down Interstate 390. "Hawaii is heaven."

He also had the privilege of working a North Carolina game that featured a freshman phenom named Michael Jordan.

"There was a play where the ball came off the backboard toward the foul line," he recalls. "Jordan took a running jump, caught the ball in mid-air and stuffed it back into the basket.

"Everyone in the place was in awe. I'm standing there looking at him. I wanted to applaud!"

6:51 p.m. About 1,500 officials work Division I basketball games, and they come from all walks of life: businessmen, police officers, former athletes. Shapiro worked Big East games for seven years but now officiates mostly games in the Atlantic 10 and Metro Atlantic Athletic Conference — about 40 per season — because of his job at MCC.

He laughs when asked how many coaches he has ejected.

"Not many," he says. "I've been fortunate."

He has even survived five encounters with Indiana's incorrigible Bobby Knight, including the Hoosiers' shocking NCAA Tournament loss to Cleveland State in 1986.

"He was first class," Shapiro says of Knight. "He made a point of coming up to us after the game and telling us what a great job we did. And that meant a lot, because that loss was crushing."

One year later, Indiana beat Syracuse on Keith Smart's last-second jumper to win the national title.

Shapiro hasn't had any run-ins with SU coach Jim Boeheim, either.

"When Jimmy started out, he was rough on officials," Shapiro says. "He's made a 100 percent turnaround. He got the label as a whiner early, but he's been terrific."

7:02 p.m. Some coaches invite trouble.

Years ago, Shapiro and fellow Rochesterian Pete Pavia were working a West Virginia-St. Bonaventure game. The visiting Bonnies trailed badly at halftime and Shapiro was approached by their coach, Tom Chapman.

"Murph, give me a technical," Chapman pleaded. "I need to fire my team up."

Shapiro was stunned.

"I looked at him like 'Give me a break,' and walked away," he says.

Five seconds into the second half, Chapman began screaming at Shapiro and received his technical. Then he turned his attention on Pavia and earned another—and an automatic ejection.

"Later, he told us that they were getting beat so badly he just wanted out," Shapiro says. "Pete and I talked and said we should have left him out there."

Of course, Chapman was only a warmup act for Pavia. The long-time official, who died of cancer in 1992, became part of a national sports story by ejecting the hallowed Smith from North Carolina's 1991 NCAA semifinal loss to Kansas.

"Dean had never been thrown out before but he deserved to get run that time," Shapiro says. "He kept repeating himself over and over, and he wouldn't let go. He was trying to show up Pete."

Pavia also tossed Georgetown coach John Thompson during a memorable Big East game at Syracuse's Carrier Dome. Thompson called Pavia two days later to apologize. Shapiro says that Smith finally telephoned Pavia when the referee was gravely ill with cancer.

Pete said "Coach I appreciate the call, but I've got many more important things on my mind," Shapiro recalls.

Officials aren't always right, but don't expect one to turn in another.

"If we know one of the other guys has blown a call, we stay away from the coach," Shapiro says. "We don't go near him. And you try to never make a call you can't explain. That gets you in more trouble than anything."

Coaches aren't the only ones on the ejection line. Henrietta's Gene Monje once tossed a Niagara priest who gave him the "choke" sign. Shapiro laughs at the memory.

"Priests can be tough!" he says.

7:28 p.m. The car turns onto Buffalo Street in Olean.

"If you can recruit here, you can recruit anywhere," Shapiro says. "It's one and a half hours from Buffalo, two from Rochester. It's tough."

The parking lot attendant outside the Reilly Center chuckles when he sees Shapiro approaching.

"Get out of here, you!" he says, motioning the familiar face forward.

Inside the cozy gym, workers are setting up the media tables while the Bonnies cheerleaders practice their routines at midcourt. Tipoff for the game, shown on ESPN2, is more than two hours away.

"We have to be here 90 minutes before the game," Shapiro says, heading to the officials room next to the gym. "But that's good. It gives us a chance to unwind and hold our pre-game meeting."

Inside the quiet locker room, a third official is lying on a couch. Ed Corbett lives in Yonkers and is a utility worker for Con Edison. He works games in the Atlantic 10, Southeastern Conference, Atlantic Coast Conference and the Big East and has taken two vacation days to work this game and the Mississippi-Tennessee SEC clash the next night. Corbett flew in to Buffalo, and then drove to Olean. After the game, he will drive back to Buffalo, sleep about four hours in a hotel, and catch a 6:30 a.m. flight to Memphis. He'll sleep a little more there and drive an hour to Oxford, Mississippi.

"It's a grind," he says.

Clark nods in agreement. He was at the Pentagon at 6:15 this morning before flying to Rochester. He'll return to Washington the next day, and then head directly to work. Shapiro has it the easiest— a 9:30 a.m. meeting at MCC.

8:01 p.m. Shapiro removes his jacket and tie and sits in a chair, sipping water. Corbett remains on the couch, while Clark sits facing them on a bench. Officials get their assignments each month and have different partners each game. Steve Campbell, the assistant athletic director at St. Bonaventure, walks in with checks for the officials. Division I refs receive from $400 (Metro Atlantic Athletic Conference) to $650 (Big East), plus travel expenses and up to $125 per diem.

There are risks besides driving in icy conditions and whiteouts. East Rochester's Carmen Urzetta recently tore up a knee officiating at Bucknell University and so he's out for the season.

Campbell informs the refs that the gym lights will be "killed" from 8:45-9:02 so that the Bonnies can unveil a new mascot.

"Rhode Island stayed in Buffalo today, so they're not going to get a shoot-around," he tells the refs. "How do you think that will go over?"

"Not very well," Corbett says.

Referees are not supposed to reveal their next assignment because the NCAA fears that gamblers will try to contact them. When do coaches learn who is officiating their game?

"Hopefully, when we walk onto the floor," Shapiro says.

But inquiring minds sometimes find out. Ten years ago, Shapiro was working a Rhode Island-St. Bonaventure game. Shapiro sported a mini-Afro back then, making him easy to spot.

"I walk onto the court, and all of a sudden I'm followed by five Bonaventure students wearing Afro wigs with T-shirts reading *Murph Shapiro's Fan Club*," he recalls.

Rhode Island coach Tom Penders shook his head, smiling.

"Yeah, I've got a chance tonight," he told Shapiro.

A reporter asks Shapiro his age, and he promptly answers, "59."

Corbett lifts his head in shock.

"You don't look a day over 51, Murph!" he says.

Shapiro looks at the reporter.

"Put down 51," he says.

8:45 p.m. Outside of the locker room, a thunderous roar goes up as the Bonnies' new wolf mascot is unveiled. Inside, the officials are talking strategy.

"Tell the players to only talk to their own team," Shapiro cautions his colleagues. "No trash talking with the opponents. This time of year, that can be dangerous."

Corbett expects an intense game.

"It's a big game, it's on TV and there's going to be a lot of emotion," he says. "We're just not going to be abused, that's all."

The refs wish each other luck.

"Let's throw a shutout tonight," Shapiro says.

There is silence. The game is still several minutes away, and now there is nothing to do but wait.

Suddenly, Shapiro pokes Clark in the foot.

"So," he says, "how do you like those shoes?"

9:12 p.m. Rhode Island runs onto the floor amid a chorus of jeers. Almost on cue, the three officials walk out of their room and onto the court. This is not by coincidence. Referees must be on the court when the teams come out to warm up.

"If someone dunks the ball, we have to call a technical," Shapiro explains.

9:36 p.m. The Atlantic 10 has named Clark the head referee for this game, and he tosses the jump ball in the air to begin play. He also blows the first whistle, a traveling call on the Bonnies two minutes into the game.

"Bull——!" the raucous crowd yells.

The first half is remarkably clean, with only four fouls called on each team. With 2:07 minutes left before intermission, Rhode Island coach Jim Harrick is practically begging the officials to call a foul on the Bonnies for aggressive play. Shapiro pulls his whistle out of his mouth long enough to say "It wasn't a foul, coach," and trots by.

Rhode Island takes a 41-25 lead into halftime.

With eight minutes left in the game, Shapiro whistles Rams center Luther Clay for an offensive charge. This delights the partisan crowd, but enrages Harrick, who grabs his right arm and yells at Shapiro. The referee shakes his head.

Shapiro later calls a foul on Rhode Island's Preston Murphy. The senior guard nods in agreement, and then he slips over to see Clark.

"Mr. Ref," he says. "How is that a foul?"

Clark can't believe his ears.

"Now why do you want to ask me about a call like that?" he says, putting his hand on the player's right shoulder. "You think I'm going to tell you something different? He was right there!"

The Rams build a commanding 62-38 lead, and Harrick is soon smiling, popping candy into his mouth, joking with his student managers and with his son and assistant, Jim Jr. The Bonnies slowly crawl back into the game and cut the lead to six in the final minute. The smile disappears from Harrick's face, and when Shapiro fails to call traveling on a Bonnies player with 40 seconds left, Harrick loses it.

"You don't know the game!" he yells, face-to-face with Shapiro.

"And you do?" Shapiro retorts before walking away.

Rhode Island holds on to win 77-70. The game's intensity picked up dramatically in the second half, with 17 fouls called. Rhode Island was whistled for 14 overall, compared to 11 for the Bonnies.

11:33 p.m. The game has been over for only five minutes, but Corbett is en route to Buffalo. Shapiro and Clark prepare for a quick shower as they review the past two hours.

"Jimmy Baron was great tonight," Shapiro says of the Bonnies' coach.

"You're right," Clark says. "Even when they came back, he was the same way."

They can't say the same about Harrick.

"He was laughing and smiling until it got close," Shapiro says. "All of a sudden he starts yelling at his team—and at us! But that's the way it is. Each game means so much to the coach. A loss is like a dagger in the heart."

Turkey subs that were left for the officials before the game remain untouched. But now Clark sticks one in his bag and Shapiro grabs the other.

"It's time to head home," Shapiro says wearily, walking into the night.

BASEBALL WIVES: DIAMONDS AND DREAMS

Published July 21, 2005

Being a baseball wife in the minor leagues means low pay, living in hotels or small apartments, and having to be ready to change cities at a moment's notice. In 2005, I profiled some of the women whose husbands were playing Triple-A baseball for the Rochester Red Wings in the International League.

CHRIS AND STACEY HEINTZ SHARED A PRECIOUS MEMORY DURING last week's All-Star break. Chris, a catcher with the Rochester Red Wings, flew to Tampa, Florida, to visit his 7½-months-pregnant wife, and the couple viewed an ultrasound in 3D.

"It was awesome," Stacey said. "You could see the baby's face! And Chris got to see the baby for the first time."

Part of Chris' job is to prevent runners from stealing bases. But that same job steals life's special moments along the way.

"It's a challenge," says Stacey, an associate head softball coach at the University of South Florida. "I feel like we're missing out on special time."

The baby is due September 1. The Red Wings' season ends five days later, but Chris will be there for the birth, playoff race or no playoff race.

"I can't miss it," he says. "I've missed so much already."

The life of a baseball wife is filled with emotions: joy when your husband succeeds, sadness when he fails, loneliness when he's on road trips, worry when he's traded, demoted or released.

"I've always said, a baseball wife is the toughest thing out of the whole situation," says interim Wings manager Rich Miller, twice divorced but still hoping to find love. "The player is doing something he loves and making money doing it. He's traveling around with his buddies, and the wives are back home."

It can be a difficult life, which is why Rachel Lucas didn't want any part of it when she met pitcher Willie Eyre in Fort Myers, Florida, back in 2001.

"She thought all baseball players were slime," says Willie, a relief pitcher for the Wings.

Rachel had heard stories about players who forgot their vows once the team hit the road.

"I didn't want to be that girl," she says.

But Willie's sincerity wore her down, and the two were married in January 2004. Their son, Jackson, was born last December 14.

Rachel has gone from baseball novice to expert. She reads stories, scans the transaction wire and listens to Red Wings games on the radio when the team is on the road. And while she jokes that she's "a single mom for eight days at a time," she enjoys the life of a baseball wife.

"Everyone's husband has a normal job where you hear about their day," she says. "I get to see it."

The lowest-paid player in the big leagues receives the minimum salary of $316,000 (or $1,756 per day). On the Triple-A Red Wings, salaries range from $1,800 to $8,000 a month.

"It can be difficult," says Kelli Tiffee, the wife of Wings third baseman Terry Tiffee. "We've been married four years, and we've only lived together for one month (during baseball season), because the finances just aren't there. It's not glamorous."

Kelli lives with Terry and Wings infielders Jason Bartlett and Luis Maza in an apartment complex outside of Rochester. Rachel and Willie Eyre live in the same complex with pitcher Dave Gassner and his fiancee and high school sweetheart, Jenny Kohl.

"Dave said he wouldn't marry me until I found out what the life is like," says Kohl, a middle-school teacher in Hortonville, Wisconsin. "Fortunately, I've had Rachel and Kelli around. They've been wonderful. They told me exactly what it would be like."

Apparently, they haven't scared her off. The Gassner-Kohl wedding is planned for December 10.

Many wives, especially the younger ones, are with their husbands all season. Some of the older ones, like outfielder Todd

Red Wings wives (and a fiancée) laugh at a 2005 game at Frontier Field. From left: Rachel Eyre, wife of pitcher Willie Eyre; Jenny Kohl, fiancée of pitcher Dave Gassner; and Kelli Tiffee, wife of infielder Terry Tiffee. Photographer: Annette Lein

Dunwoody's wife Jessica, join their husbands when their kids are out of school in May or June.

For some, the wait is even longer. Pitching coach Bobby Cuellar saw wife Nora during last week's All-Star break — for the first time since February.

When the Wings hit the road, often for eight days at a time, the wives settle into a routine.

"We play cards, scrapbook and listen to every game," Rachel Eyre says. "And we go to the mall a lot. The first couple of days are OK. By the end, we're ready for them to come home."

Rachel was a teacher before she gave birth last December. Now Jackson keeps her plenty busy during the day. Often the wives do not work during the season because of the unpredictability of their husbands' profession.

The wives talk to their spouses several times a day. In the past, this would mean unusually high phone bills, but free person-to-person cell phone plans have allowed the Wings players and their spouses to speak frequently, whether the team is in Durham, Toledo, Louisville or Pawtucket.

Willie and Rachel Eyre speak eight or nine times a day. Chris and Stacey Heintz also burn up the lines.

"I don't listen to the games on the Internet," Stacey says. "I enjoy it more when Chris calls and tells me about the game and how he did."

Kelli Tiffee says the biggest misconception the public has is that it's a "glamorous life."

"He plays every single day," she says. "Holidays, weekends, there's no break. And if you don't get called up (to the majors), financially it's not there."

Trust is a key ingredient in any successful marriage, and it's crucial in baseball, when the spouses are separated for weeks or months at a time. Stories of infidelity have been well documented, and the baseball divorce rate is high.

"It's a concern," Miller says. "I've seen some nasty fights — wives fooling around, husbands fooling around."

A few years ago, a fight broke out between two women who were waiting for a Red Wings outfielder outside the clubhouse at Frontier Field. The women had introduced themselves. It turned out that one was the player's wife, the other was his girlfriend.

The Red Wings wives interviewed for this story say they trust their husbands implicitly.

"It's complete trust," Rachel Eyre says.

"We're lucky," Kelli Tiffee adds. "We have good guys."

Because of her busy job as a college softball coach, Stacey Heintz doesn't see her husband from spring training until the end of South Florida's season in late May. Then she tries to make one visit a month until the Wings' season concludes on Labor Day.

"We make up for it in the winter," she says.

It's different this year. Stacey can't travel because of her pregnancy, so she won't see Chris until it's time to have the baby. Still, she doesn't worry about any hanky-panky going on.

"Chris is a special guy," she says. "There's never been a time that it bothered me. What bothers me is that we can't be together more."

Chris says it would be "very difficult" for him to stray, given how often the couple talk.

"I call her at 9 when I wake up, at 11:30 (p.m.) after a game and a lot in between," he says. "You'd have to be pretty sneaky to do something like that."

Miller was married briefly in the 1970s and again from 1981 to 2003. He says baseball played a role in both breakups.

"I think taking care of the house, the kids growing up and having to make some decisions without me contributed to it over time," he says. "It's not an easy life."

A baseball wife must be ready to pick up and leave at a moment's notice. At any given time, her husband could be promoted, demoted, traded or released. Last winter, LeAnn Baker checked out hospitals in Rochester and Minneapolis. She's expecting her first child in August and wasn't sure where her husband, Wings pitcher Scott Baker, would be playing. She still doesn't know. Baker was promoted to the Twins earlier this month, sent back to Rochester for one game, called up again to pitch Saturday against Detroit, and may return to Rochester next week. Or not.

"I told my wife about it when we were dating," Willie Eyre says. "She said, 'How long do they give you to get there, a week?' I said, 'A few hours.'" He's not kidding. If a Red Wing is promoted to the Twins on Monday at 10 p.m., he's expected to join the parent club the next day, whether it's in New York or Anaheim, California.

"The worst part is the packing and unpacking and packing again," Rachel Eyre says.

Last year, Kelli Tiffee witnessed a special moment when she saw Wings manager Phil Roof tell her husband that he was going to the big leagues for the first time.

"I could read Phil's lips," she says. "It was awesome."

Terry left the next day. Kelli packed that night, then drove 16 hours the next morning.

"I heard his first game on the radio," she says. "It was so exciting I had to pull over!"

This year, Terry was promoted on April 13, but Kelli knew it was a short-term situation until Twins catcher Joe Mauer was healthy. "I waited it out here," she says.

When Tiffee was recalled on May 5, however, Kelli went to Minneapolis with him. This promotion lasted a month.

"I like to pack everything," she says, "but I'm finally down to one suitcase."

Heintz is having a terrific season, hitting .308 and recently earning International League Batter of the Week honors. Still, the 10-year minor leaguer wonders how much longer he'll want to live apart from his wife — and his future child.

"It's something I'll have to evaluate in the off-season," he says. "The off-season is makeup time for us, but before you know it, it's spring training again and you're gone."

The baseball life is not for everyone, but many embrace it.

"The ups and downs are tough," Rachel Eyre says. "Fortunately, Willie doesn't bring the wins and losses home with him."

Neither does Gassner, but his fiancee isn't as laid-back.

"I want to be out there playing, where I can control things," Jenny Kohl says. "I played college softball and coached. I like to be in control."

Adding to the stress of a baseball life are the unusual hours. The Wings play most of their games at night, so they often sleep in and then have to be at the ballpark by 3 p.m.

"Lunch time is the best time," Kelli Tiffee says. "We have about three hours before he has to go to the park."

Even the offseason doesn't guarantee time together. Last winter, Eyre and Tiffee played in Venezuela and Gassner went to the Dominican Republic. Their significant others stayed home.

They're in this for the same reason. They dream of finding financial security in the majors. In the meantime, it's a challenging but fascinating life.

"I think about Jackson," Rachel Eyre says. "I think it's going to be so neat for him to see his dad play ball. I mean, there are salesmen, reporters and other people who are on the road and don't see their families. How many kids can say their dad is a professional baseball player?"

WALK-ONS: NOTHING FOR MONEY

Published December 26, 1997

*Everyone knows about the All-American high school basketball players
who go on to play for major college teams on full scholarships.
But what about the walk-ons, who make the team with no scholarship
money and very little chance of playing? I decided to find out.*

"Of course we shower after the game. We've warmed up harder
than anybody."
  —Georgia Tech basketball walk-on James Gaddy in 1991

CHARLIE LOCKWOOD WAS A FOUR-TIME ALL-AMERICAN LACROSSE
player at Syracuse University, and helped the Orangemen win a
national title. Last year, he played on a Rochester Knighthawks club
that captured the Major Indoor Lacrosse League championship. But
when sports fans spot Lockwood, they usually have only one thing
on their minds.

"Everyone wants to talk about the 3-pointer I hit against
Tennessee," Lockwood says, laughing. "I did all that in lacrosse,
and the only thing people care about is my one great moment
in basketball."

Lockwood was a multisport star at West Genesee High School in
Syracuse. He was good enough in basketball to be recruited by several
Division II and III teams, but great enough in lacrosse to earn a full
ride to perennial power SU. Lockwood satisfied his sports fantasy the
way hundreds of college students do each year: he became a walk-on.

The position is strictly voluntary and is common to virtually all
sports that offer scholarships. A walk-on is not recruited or awarded
an athletic scholarship. He or she simply . . . walks on.

"They are invaluable," says Syracuse University basketball Jim
Boeheim, a one-time walk-on at SU. "With our limited number of
scholarships, we can't get through practice without walk-ons."

Division I programs are allowed to offer 85 football scholarships, 13 for men's basketball (down from 20 in Boeheim's playing days) and 15 for women's basketball. The rest of the roster is filled out by walk-ons, many of whom could be big fish in the small ponds of Division III.

They choose instead to toil for big-time schools with little time on the court or field.

Chris Edwards was cut from the East High varsity basketball team in Rochester, New York, in his junior year, and then didn't even bother to try out as a senior. He didn't get mad — he made a Division I college team.

Edwards is the lone walk-on at Niagara University. His job is to play on the "scout" team in practice, running opponents' plays. So far, his game experience has been confined to an exhibition against Brock (Ontario) College.

"It means a lot to me being on this team," says Edwards, a computer science major. "My dad passed away in August, and I want to make him proud."

The 6-foot- 4 Edwards played volleyball for East and spent many days shooting hoops at the North Street Recreation Center. He also played with his two older brothers in the annual Teddi T basketball tournament downtown.

Unlike walk-ons from national powerhouses such as Syracuse, Edwards does not join the team on plane trips and does not receive scholarship money. But he is a Purple Eagle in every other way.

"I put in just as much time as the starters," he says. "And I work just as hard."

Lockwood became close friends with Syracuse assistant basketball coach Bernie Fine, and one day during Lockwood's senior year, Fine urged the lacrosse star to try out for the team. So Lockwood did, along with 50 other wannabes at the cramped Manley Field House.

"Three of us made it," says Lockwood, now a Syracuse stockbroker for Paine Webber. "I think it helped that I had already passed my physical (for lacrosse)."

When SU opened the 1993-94 season at the Carrier Dome against Tennessee, Lockwood told his parents to tape the game on ESPN.

"You might catch me sitting on the bench," he told them.

They caught much more. With the Orange crushing the Volunteers, Boeheim put Lockwood into the game in the waning minutes.

"I hadn't even taped my ankles," Lockwood says. "(Point guard) Adrian Autry told me, 'As soon as you catch the ball, shoot it.'"

Instead, Lockwood passed off to Lawrence Moten.

"I said 'Shoot it,'" Autry sternly reminded his new teammate.

So the next time Lockwood got the ball, he launched a 3-pointer from the left side. Swish.

"The crowd really went wild, I guess because I was a hometown kid," Lockwood says. "After the game, I turned around at my locker and there were 15 reporters there. The story even made *USA Today*."

Boeheim laughs when recalling the shot and calls it "one of my favorite walk-on memories."

Lockwood played in nine more games and scored just six more points. But his '3' follows him around wherever he goes.

"Sometimes I'll read to kids at schools," Lockwood says. "When I ask if they have any questions, all these hands shoot up. They want to know what it was like to play basketball for SU."

The Nebraska football team is a genuine powerhouse, with two national titles and a permanent spot in the Top 25 under retiring coach Tom Osborne. Lesser-known is "Dr. Tom's" secret prescription for success: walk-ons. Most Big 12 rosters include about 100 players. Nebraska's fluctuates between 150 and 175, meaning half of the team is composed of walk-ons.

"Coach Osborne and his staff like to have a lot of players," sports information director Keith Mann says. "We're the only Division I school in the state, and I'd say 85 percent of our walk-ons are local kids."

One major reason is that tuition is cheaper for Nebraska residents who attend an in-state school. But there is opportunity in Huskerland. Many walk-ons go on to earn scholarships, including former flashy tailback I.M. Hipp, current starting fullback Joel Makovicka, and John Parrella, now a starting defensive tackle with the NFL's San Diego Chargers.

Of the 84 players on Nebraska's preseason depth chart, 32 originally were walk-ons.

Most are usually scout players who play various roles in practice. Some leave a lasting impact.

Midway through the 1994 season, No. 2 Nebraska lost starting quarterback Tommie Frazier to a blood clot in his leg, and backup Brook Berringer to a collapsed lung. Enter Matt Turman, a sophomore walk-on. Turman replaced Berringer during the Huskers' game with Oklahoma State and drove them to two touchdowns in a 32-3 romp. The following week, he started against No. 16 Kansas State. His job consisted primarily of handing the ball off to tailback Lawrence Phillips, who gained 126 yards.

Turman completed 2 of 4 passes for 15 yards before injuring his arm. Nebraska won 17-6 and went on to claim its first of two consecutive national championships.

If Nebraska wins for quantity, give the Florida Gators first prize for quality walk-ons. Ten Gators have gone from nonscholarship to the National Football League.

Kerwin Bell showed up uninvited in 1983. He returned the following year and, still without a scholarship, was named Southeastern Conference Player of the Year. Bell earned a scholarship and finished his career as Florida's all-time leading passer with more than 7,500 yards. He was a Heisman Trophy candidate his senior year.

Defensive back Louis Oliver came to Gainesville as a walk-on. He left as the No. 1 draft pick of the Miami Dolphins in 1989.

Jeff Hornacek was working for a paper cup company in the summer of 1981 when he decided to give basketball another chance. The 6-foot-4 guard from LaGrange, Illinois, enrolled at Iowa State for the spring 1982 semester and worked out with the Cyclones basketball team at point guard. He was so impressive that coach Johnny Orr gave him a scholarship. Hornacek was elected co-captain his junior and senior years, and set Big Eight records for assists in a season (108) and career (337). Hornacek was chosen by the Phoenix Suns in the 1986 National Basketball Association draft. He was an all-star in 1992 before being traded to Philadelphia for Charles Barkley. He now plays for the Utah Jazz.

It's rare that a walk-on becomes a basketball star like Hornacek. It's even rarer that he eventually becomes the school's highly successful coach for more than two decades. With his round glasses and thin frame, Jim Boeheim looked more like Buddy Holly than budding basketball star when he stepped onto the SU campus in 1962.

Boeheim had enjoyed a terrific high school career at Lyons, about an hour west of Syracuse, where he was an all-state selection. He was recruited by Division I Colgate but chose to take his chances at Syracuse. Boeheim was the sixth man on the Orangemen's freshman team — first-year students weren't allowed to play varsity then — and was so impressive that he earned a scholarship and a spot on the SU team the following year.

As a senior, Boeheim averaged 14.6 points and became just the 10th Orangeman to score more than 400 points in a season. He finished with a 9.8 career scoring average and was the last cut of the Chicago Bulls in the NBA draft. In 1972, Boeheim became an assistant coach at SU under Roy Danforth, and then took over the program four years later. The walk-on from Lyons has recorded more than 500 wins as coach and taken SU to two national championship games.

Boeheim admittedly has a soft spot for walk-ons — his roster this year includes 5-foot-6 Jason Mallin — and often finds a way to give them at least a partial scholarship.

"They don't get a lot of publicity or playing time, and you rarely have one that becomes a star," he says, "but I can't say enough about walk-ons. They mean a lot to us."

Rudy Ruettiger was 5-foot-6 and finished third from the bottom of his high school class in Joliet, Illinois. Playing football at Notre Dame wasn't a dream, it was a hallucination. At least that's what Ruettiger's friends told him.

But after being turned down by Notre Dame three times, working in a factory and attending junior college, he finally was admitted to the world's most famous college and landed on the football team as a walk-on. For two years, he held blocking dummies and ran scout plays while consistently pushing coach Dan Devine to let him dress for a game.

It finally happened on November 8, 1975, against Georgia Tech. On the game's final play, Devine sent Ruettiger in.

The opposing linemen laughed at the munchkin, until Ruettiger raced in untouched and sacked the Georgia Tech quarterback. The Notre Dame players, including a quarterback named Joe Montana, hoisted Ruettiger on their shoulders — a first for the storied program. It was literally a Hollywood ending. In 1993, *Rudy* became the feel-good movie of the year.

Walk-ons everywhere cheered.

JOURNEYMEN PLAYERS: FOR LOVE OF THE GAME

Published August 14, 1994

What's it like to be a journeyman baseball player trapped in the minors?
I asked several veterans who were still chasing the dream.

HE HAS WRITTEN THEIR NAMES ON HIS GLOVE, SPIKES, WRIST bands, batting gloves and the bill of his cap. He has taped their picture inside his cap, too. Wherever he plays, there are Torey and Casey at the bat.

"Everybody has a certain reason for playing," Jeff Schaefer said by phone from Tacoma, Washington, where he plays shortstop for the Triple-A Tigers. "This is motivation for me. These are my daughters, and I never let them slip my mind."

Schaefer forces a laugh.

"I used to have my wife's name everywhere too," he says.

The nine-year marriage to Kim ended last summer, but the separation began long before that. A ballplayer and a flight attendant might be the perfect combination for frequent flier mileage, but it puts an instant strain on a marriage.

"We were never together," said Schaefer, who has played for 13 teams in his 14-year career, including two stints with the Rochester Red Wings. "When you're a ballplayer, you're alone a lot and you don't really get to know the other person. It's easy to drift apart."

The anguish Schaefer feels is common to players in every town that embraces a professional team, ballplayers who try to reconcile their boyhood fantasies-come-true with the adult realities they face as husbands and fathers.

"It's a great life, but it's also a rough life," says former Red Wings pitcher Anthony Telford, now with the Richmond Braves. "And if you don't find someone who is understanding and who is willing to made the adjustment, it can be terrible."

Telford got married in 1988, five months after he began his pro career with the Newark Orioles.

"When I was in Newark, Christine was home in California," he says. "Ever since, she's lived in whatever town I've played in. Being together is the most important thing."

It's the one thing Schaefer can't have with his daughters.

Schaefer played for Rochester in 1984-85, and again for the first month of this season. He was released by the Baltimore Orioles on May 2 and landed a minor league job with the Oakland Athletics in Tacoma. Now he is closer to the majors — he had a brief stint this summer and expected another call-up before the players' strike — but farther than ever from his daughters, who live with their mom in Tampa, Florida.

"Torey was with me most of the summer," says Schaefer. "But I haven't seen Casey since March."

Torey is 9, Casey 6. They are too young to fully comprehend why their father is three time zones away, but Schaefer is devoted to someday explaining it to them. Each night, he writes in the journal he keeps on his computer.

"Sometimes I have a conversation with them, and sometimes I have one with myself," he says. "I'm keeping this diary so that someday maybe they'll understand why things were this way."

Schaefer often speaks to groups about the life of a ballplayer. He doesn't mince words.

"The common fan thinks this is such a glamorous life," he says. "They don't know about playing in towns where it costs $800 a month for an apartment, and you're making $1,600 a month. And they don't know about having to pack late at night and drive 14 hours to be in a new city the next day.

"I'm chasing a dream, and there's a price to pay. I hear about plays, about riding a bike for the first time. Those are the painful things."

It was time to leave, but Jeff Manto stood frozen in the doorway of his home in suburban Philadelphia in May. Two days before, Manto's wife had given birth to the couple's first child. Manto hates flying, but he had enjoyed the ride of his life while zooming in from Columbus, Ohio, for the big event.

"I couldn't wait," he said. "It was something I'd waited for all my life." The weekend was perfect, with Jeff and Denise showing off little Gabrielle for family and friends and bonding with their new daughter.

Now it was Sunday night, and Manto was headed back to Rochester to play third base for the Wings.

"When we gave birth, I actually forgot what my job was," Manto said. "All of a sudden, I was just a father. But when I had to leave the house, I sat there and cried in front of my wife. And I apologized to her. I didn't want to go. I didn't want to come back here."

It's 11 weeks later, and Manto's family has since joined him in Rochester. He still goes away for road trips, but he spends every idle moment with the two women in his life. Being a family man has changed Manto's view of the game he loves.

"I used to play for selfish reasons: to get to the big leagues, to be one of the best players," he said. "I still play with just as much pride, but there's something more fulfilling when I leave the park."

Three years ago, there wasn't.

"Before I got married, I left the park and had nothing," Manto said. "I couldn't wait to play again, because that's all there was in my life. Now if I have a bad night, it doesn't eat at me like it used to. I go home and I have a beautiful wife and a beautiful daughter. That means more than any home run ever could."

During his Hall of Fame induction speech July 31, Steve Carlton said a baseball wife had the "toughest assignment in life." That point was driven home to Lou Ann Dostal last December.

"Bruce left for Venezuela (winter ball) December 20," she recalled during a recent game at Silver Stadium. "I spent Christmas with my family, but it didn't feel like Christmas at all. It was horrible."

So Lou Ann boarded a plane and joined her husband, a second-year Red Wings outfielder, in Venezuela on New Year's Day.

"We didn't exchange gifts for Christmas," she said. "We used our Christmas money on the trip, and I stayed a week."

When Lou Ann wasn't in Venezuela, she was calling there. One phone bill came to $700 (their monthly bills now are about $100).

"We tried to be good about it, but we ended up talking every day," Lou Ann said.

Bruce never intended to find his wife so early in life.

"I thought I would play the field, have some fun," he said.

That changed one day in November 1987, when he met Lou Ann DeZao in a New Jersey hair salon.

"He came in to say hello to someone he knew," Lou Ann said. "I wound up cutting his hair."

Bruce was caught looking, and a relationship developed that winter.

"I had no idea what he meant when he said he was a minor league baseball player," Lou Ann said. "But March came and spring training, and I was like, 'Oh, this means you're leaving me?'"

Dostal, then a Los Angeles Dodgers farmhand, spent the 1988 season playing for Bakersfield in the Class A California League. Long distance was the next best thing to being there, and the Dostals' phone bill resembled a mortgage payment.

"It was a tough year," Bruce said. "I only saw her twice, and she gave me an ultimatum before the next season: 'Give me a ring, or I might not be here.'"

The Dostals were married in February 1990, but Bruce split that season between Vero Beach, California, and San Antonio. Months later, he was acquired by the Philadelphia Phillies and finally began living in the same time zone as his wife. Dostal joined the Wings early last season, and Lou Ann has kept the same routine ever since.

She lives in Parsippany, New Jersey, with her brother and sister-in-law and their three children. She works all week in her boutique, and then drives to Rochester when the Wings are home on weekends and stays with Bruce in his $650-a-month apartment in Webster.

Children have become a high priority.

"At first, I didn't want to have kids until I was settled someplace," Bruce said. "I didn't want them to live the life of a ballplayer, always on the move."

But Dostal realizes he may never put down roots as long as he is a Triple-A player. A brief call-up to the Baltimore Orioles this season rejuvenated his zest for the game, and Dostal expects to be in some team's camp next March.

Wings left fielder Jim Wawruck has risen steadily through the

Orioles' farm system the past four years, and Marnie Laubach has been there every step of the way. They met while attending separate colleges in Vermont, and Wawruck remembers the first time Marnie got a taste of baseball life.

"It was my rookie year and she was staying home in Vermont," Wawruck recalled. "She flew down to visit me in Florida, and I had to go to Frederick, Maryland, that same day. She'd never been to Florida, and she had to pack up and leave."

Marnie lives with Jim in Rochester and works as a nanny for a 6-month-old baby. Marriage is likely, but Wawruck hopes he is in a more secure position — left field for the Orioles would be nice — by the time the nuptials take place.

"I don't want any distractions until I get where I want to be," he said. "We're both really happy right now, and that's why she's so great. Anyone else would have probably been gone by now."

Damon Buford was 6 when his father, Don, retired from baseball. Damon was too young to remember the life his family led with Dad on the road, including four seasons in Japan, but he's all too familiar with the routine now.

Buford, 24, has been around enough players to know there's a life in the fast lane off the diamond as well.

"It's a hard life," said Buford, who is single. "There was a Players' Association study in the '70s about divorce rates of ballplayers and it was some huge figure, like 75 percent. You've got to find a companion who is strong mentally."

Finding that person is especially difficult in the minors, Buford said.

"You're down, up, down, up. You can literally be in any city or league the next day."

The life of a major league ballplayer can be tremendous, with an average salary of $1.2 million, fame and four months off in the winter. Life in the minors is a struggle, and many players have off-season jobs to supplement their income. Money is tight and living arrangements can be a bit cramped.

"When I was in 'A' ball, I was only making $850 a month," Telford said. "We lived in Frederick, Maryland, in a townhouse that cost $850 a month."

The Telfords obviously couldn't afford the rent, so they asked a few friends to move in. Actually, they asked five, including New York Mets first baseman David Segui and his wife.

"There were seven of us in a three-bedroom townhouse," Telford said. "Picture five people trying to cook after a game, or seven people trying to watch a 19-inch TV. We got real close."

Telford firmly believes that support at home is more important than support on the diamond.

"The only way you can be successful in this game, and I'll take this to my grave, is if you have a wife who is willing to accept the lifestyle and keep her faith in you. Baseball is a selfish game. It's inconvenient and often it's no fun with the traveling and stuff. We're all going after a dream, but the dream doesn't mean anything if the person you love doesn't share it."

4

FROM ALL WALKS OF LIFE

THE O'ROURKES:
LIKE FATHER, LIKE SON

Published December 25, 1999

This is one of my favorite stories I've ever written, in large part because I have so much respect and admiration for the O'Rourke family, but also because I have a personal connection with them. Read about two legendary coaches who touched sports in a small town in suburban Rochester, New York, for more than half a century.

"Billy's the kind of guy who says, 'If you knock a guy down, help him up.' Mr. O'Rourke (Sr.) was the kind who said, 'If you knock a guy down, help him up. And then knock him down again.'"

— Jim Klimschot, former Webster High point guard

THE VOICE ECHOES FROM THE TOP ROW OF BLEACHERS AT THE Webster High School gymnasium.

"Call it! Call it!" Bill O'Rourke Sr. screams at the basketball referees below, a game program wrapped tightly in his right hand.

The referee instead makes a call against the Webster varsity and O'Rourke slumps against the wall.

"Oh, come off it!" he says.

He is 76 now. His voice is thinner, his hair lighter than when he roamed the Webster sidelines from 1950-78. He has been battling prostate cancer, and last April doctors inserted a pacemaker into the man known for his generous heart.

But the fire still burns.

O'Rourke won 343 games and one Section V title in Rochester before turning over the job to his son, Bill Jr., who has won 293 games and another sectional crown in 22 seasons.

Fifty years. Six hundred thirty-six wins.

"Two great men," says Clark Cogan, who starred on the 1972 Webster team and whose son Rhian is a junior forward for the current Warriors. "Coach O'Rourke wanted to win badly, but he also realized we were going to go on and do other things in our lives. He spent a lot of time making sure we were good human beings. Junior is the exact same way."

The O'Rourkes are as much a part of Webster as Hegedorn's, a supermarket in town since 1953, or the welcome sign that proudly states "Webster: Where Life Is Worth Living."

"These are two of the finest men I've ever known," says Doug Klick, a longtime friend of both O'Rourkes. "They are Webster basketball."

The O'Rourke formula is a simple one, Senior says: "Be a gentleman — but a tough gentleman."

Bill O'Rourke Sr. was born and raised in Ilion, a small town near Utica, New York. A veteran of the Marines, he attended St. Lawrence University on the G.I. Bill and led the basketball team in scoring for three years. He also worked in a Canton, New York, liquor store for 40 cents an hour to support wife Loretta — his high school sweetheart — and baby son Bill Jr. When O'Rourke graduated with a business degree in 1950, he was hired to replace James Smith as coach of the Webster varsity. His salary was $2,700. He was only 27, but he left no doubt about who was in charge.

"Oh, he was tough," says Gerry Coxford, a senior guard on that first O'Rourke team. "If you did something he didn't like, he'd put you on the bench and forget you were there."

O'Rourke's dream season was 1960-61, when the Ridgemen beat defending champion Franklin 50-41 in the Section V Class A championship to finish 21-0.

"He was the commander-in-chief of the forces," says John Ladwig, the center on that great team. "He did it his way."

The Ridgemen were good, and they were cocky — too cocky for O'Rourke. Two nights before the showdown with Franklin, the coach sprang a surprise on his team. He brought a dozen former St. Lawrence University players to Webster's practice for an impromptu scrimmage — with O'Rourke as referee.

Bill O'Rourke Sr. makes his customary visit to the Webster High locker room to go over the game with his son, Bill O'Rourke Jr., in December 1999. Webster beat Penfield to remain undefeated. Photographer: Jamie Germano

"That darn guy would've liked to kill us," Ladwig says. "All we did was run, with hardly any water breaks. He had someone running the scoreboard and everything." The Ridgemen met their match that evening.

"Those old guys beat the living hell out of us," Ladwig says. "It taught us we weren't invincible."

Two nights later, unbeaten Franklin High paid the price. Three years ago, a panel of veteran area coaches and officials voted those '61 Ridgemen the best basketball team in Section V history.

But memories were short — and tempers shorter — back then. When Webster finished 1-17 three years later — with a young roster that included junior guard Bill O'Rourke Jr. — some town citizens lobbied for O'Rourke's dismissal.

"They called me many names, and none of them resembled

'Coach,'" Senior says. "It didn't bother me — much."

The following season, with virtually the same roster, Webster won the Monroe County West championship with a 15-5 record and advanced to the sectional semifinals. Years later, O'Rourke was a character witness in a trial. The defense attorney began his questioning by saying, "Now Mr. O'Rourke, you're a great basketball coach, aren't you?"

O'Rourke didn't miss a beat.

"It depends on who you ask — and when," he responded.

The jury erupted in laughter.

O'Rourke would lead Webster to the title game four more times, but lose in 1970, '72, '75 and '78. In terms of anguish, nothing compares to '72. Webster built a nine-point lead late in the Section V Class AA championship, but Rush-Henrietta kept getting closer, closer ... The Comets finally won, 53-51, on a basket by freshman Steve Bailey with one second remaining.

"It was the greatest heartbreak of my career," Senior says. "I still think about it."

Ron Malley, Webster's junior varsity coach for 12 years following Senior's retirement, nods in agreement from the bleachers.

"He talked about it on the way over here to the game," Malley says. "That game haunts him."

By 1978, O'Rourke was ready to bow out. Webster had split into two high schools five years before — Thomas and Schroeder — and his duties as Webster's supervisor of attendance and director of census were keeping him busy. He also wanted Billy, his junior varsity coach for the previous seven seasons, to get his chance at coaching the varsity. O'Rourke made his decision known early in the season. There was no dress code for bus trips, but on February 10, the Thomas varsity showed up wearing three-piece suits for a road game at Brockport in a tribute to their departing coach.

"They told me they wanted to go in feeling like class and leave feeling like class," O'Rourke said. "I was so proud."

The Ridgemen conducted a special ceremony at the last home game, presenting O'Rourke with a rocking chair. They then proceeded to postpone his retirement by marching through the Section V tournament before losing to East High in the championship.

"You could tell it bothered the seniors to lose the last game he coached," says John Fullerton, a freshman on that team and an All-Greater Rochester point guard in 1981. "They hurt for him, because they wanted to do it. We all did."

Senior's final record was 343-193.

The job was officially open to anyone inside the school district, but Junior was the only applicant — and the only logical choice. In May 1978, at age 31, he took over the Webster Thomas varsity.

Everything you've heard about Bill O'Rourke Jr. is true. He doesn't smoke, drink or swear. And in 22 years of coaching, he has received two technical fouls.

"It's not phony, it's who he is," says younger brother Tom, himself a two-time All-Greater Rochester star for Webster and still the school's all-time points leader. "When I was best man at his wedding, I told him to raise a glass of milk instead of champagne."

Junior has been a Spanish teacher in the Webster school district since 1969, and a "helping teacher" and interim seventh-grade principal in recent years. His hobbies include collecting baseball cards (he has more than 20,000, including a 1953 Willie Mays) and books (he has more than 500 and loves historical literature). And yes, he attends church regularly.

Billy was a shooting guard at Webster for two seasons, averaging 18 and 20 points at a time when there was no 3-point line. He was among the last of the two-hand set-shot artists and "the best pure shooter I ever had," his dad says.

Junior spent a semester at the College of Wooster (Ohio) before transferring to St. John Fisher. During his senior year, he was drafted in the 11th round of the National Basketball Association draft by the New York Knicks.

Fisher's coach, Bobby Wanzer, was a teammate of Knicks coach Red Holzman on the 1950-51 NBA champion Rochester Royals and told Holzman about his shooting star. O'Rourke appreciated being selected but decided to build a teaching career instead of trying to unseat Walt Frazier or Dick Barnett in New York.

"I could shoot as well as anyone in the NBA," he says, "but you need to do a lot more than shoot to succeed at that level."

In what might have been a first, O'Rourke sent Holzman a courtesy note, telling him he had "no illusions" about being an NBA player.

O'Rourke is unfailingly polite. Klimschot calls him "the most humble man you'll ever meet."

One day in 1983, O'Rourke and guard Terry Denson were walking into Midtown Plaza, a mall in downtown Rochester, for a radio interview, when the crowd behind them suddenly swelled.

"Mr. O'Rourke opened the door and held it for about 35 people," Denson recalled. "We were almost late for the interview."

The 1982-83 Thomas team gave Junior his greatest moment as a coach, upsetting East High 45-44 in the Section V Class AAA final for Webster's first basketball championship since Senior's 1960-61 team went undefeated.

"No more doubting Thomas" blared the next day's headline in the *Democrat and Chronicle* newspaper.

"We had four or five football players on that team (including future National Football League tight end Pat Kelly)," Junior says. "They worked so hard and just refused to lose."

Meanwhile, O'Rourke refused to swear. Former players say the harshest words they heard from their coach were "Jiminy Crickets," "asinine" and "pussycats."

"It's not a hard image to live up to," says Junior, who has three daughters with wife Dottie. "It's the way I choose to live."

"He's for real," says daughter Sarah, a senior swimmer at Webster. "I can't remember the last time he yelled at us."

Success and improvement always have been more important to him than wins. When he ran summer camps in the 1970s and '80s — at the height of the Thomas-Schroeder rivalry — he worked with the same Schroeder players who would try to steal town bragging rights from his team that winter.

The Lions never did. Thomas finished unbeaten in a decade of competition against Schroeder before the schools merged in 1983.

If Junior despises anything, it's showboating by his players. "There's no need for it," he says. "Do the job. Act like you've done it before."

Steve Dewey, a three-year Webster starter in the mid-1980s, says Junior wouldn't tolerate showoffs even behind closed doors.

"One time we were practicing and one of the guys did a nice behind-the-back pass," Dewey says. "And we scored on it."

Whistle. Stop play. "Take a seat," O'Rourke told the Magic Johnson wannabe. "Don't be a hot dog!"

Another time, Fullerton dove for a loose ball at Greece Olympia and fired a behind-the-back pass to Tony Washington for an easy layup.

"Right away I told Mr. O'Rourke, 'Sorry about that,'" says Fullerton, the only person to play for all three O'Rourkes (Tom was his eighth-grade coach). "He answered back, 'You had no choice.' It was ingrained in us."

Don't be confused. Junior is a nice guy who wants to finish first. His record is 293-158 and every loss has been difficult on him.

"I want to win just as badly as my dad did," he says, "but I keep it all inside." Then he laughs.

"I think Dad's way was healthier."

But he refuses to win at all costs. In 1986, Aquinas showed up for its Section V semifinal against Webster wearing the wrong-colored uniforms. Game officials told O'Rourke that his team was entitled to five technical foul shots — one for each Aquinas starter. He declined.

"The game should be played and won on the court," he said. "Webster wants to be remembered as a classy team, not a team that will do anything to win a game."

Aquinas won, 63-60.

"I was so proud of him for that," Senior says. "And let me tell you something: He did the right thing."

Bill and Loretta O'Rourke have been married for 53 years.

"She's still the prettiest girl I've ever seen," Senior says. "I got lucky."

Loretta was the unsung hero in the family. There would be nights when Billy was playing at Fisher and Tom was playing at Webster. Loretta would drive to Fisher for the first half, then drive back to Webster for the second half — no matter how bad the

weather. Last December, Bill and Loretta moved from their house on
Wall Road, their home since 1959, into an apartment in Webster. Bill
walks 40 minutes each day, spends countless hours doting on his
seven grandchildren, and occasionally shows up for open gyms in
Webster, where he instructs the JV and varsity players.

"Whoa, look at that!" he tells a visitor as a Webster JV player
pump fakes and scores. "I taught him that move three weeks ago!"

Then he yells toward the court.

"Way to go, babe!"

Senior attends every varsity basketball home game. Junior, who
calls his dad his "role model," wouldn't have it any other way.

"Billy will look for his dad to make sure he's there," Malley says.
"When I was coaching and his dad was late, Billy would always ask,
'Is he here yet? Is he here?'

"It's not that he needed him to help coach. He just wants him
around."

Junior has no timetable for when he will step away from coaching,
but says it will be sooner rather than later. His career is moving more
toward the role of administrator, and he points out, "The last full-
time administrator to coach in Webster was my dad, 22 years ago."

The O'Rourkes share the same basketball philosophy: run, run,
run. Their winning percentage is similar — .640 for Senior, .650 for
Junior — but the coaching styles differ in one respect.

"Dad was more fiery," Tom O'Rourke says. "Billy has always
been very much under control."

Senior baited officials with the best of them, sometimes offering
his glasses as visual aids.

"I think he was a frustrated official who always wanted to wear a
striped shirt under his suit," jokes Rush-Henrietta coach Jim Cox, a
23-year veteran.

Not his son.

"Billy knew the names of every ref, but he always called them
'Mister,'" Malley says. "He called me 'Mister' the first six years I
coached. I finally had to corner him and tell him to knock it off!"

As Malley tells his story from the Webster bleachers, Senior is
animatedly cheering on the Warriors below. With 2:37 remaining,

Webster leads Brockport by 20 points.

"When can we relax?" Malley asks O'Rourke. "My ribs are black and blue from sitting next to you."

"Not yet," O'Rourke responds, eyes glued to the game.

Just then, senior guard Sean Menz steps to the free-throw line and nails his first shot.

"I think we're in pretty good shape," O'Rourke says calmly.

Webster wins by 30.

A few minutes later, Senior walks into the locker room and shakes hands with his son.

"Nice job," he tells him.

"Thanks, Dad," his son responds.

EPILOGUE

The phone rings the next morning.

"I talked to Billy today," Senior tells a friend. "Gosh, the kids played great last night, didn't they?

"You know, Billy doesn't need my help, but I'm there whenever he does. I've told him that. He knows that."

The fire still burns.

AN UMPIRE'S LIFE: YOU'RE IN, OR 'YER OUT!'

Published August 31, 2003

I had always been interested in seeing what a professional umpire goes through, especially at the minor league level. One day, late in the 2003 season, International League ump Darren Spagnardi showed me.

DARREN SPAGNARDI WALKS INTO THE UMPIRES' ROOM IN THE basement of Frontier Field in downtown Rochester, New York, and says hello to crewmates Dan Cricks and Troy Fullwood. It's 6:20, and the start of this evening's Triple-A baseball game between the Rochester Red Wings and the Louisville Bats is being delayed by rain.

"Guys, I have some good news and some bad news," says Spagnardi, the crew chief. "I'm going up. I leave for Cincinnati tomorrow."

There's a pause, and then Cricks and Fullwood shake Spagnardi's hand. "Way to go, man," Fullwood says.

Spagnardi's absence means a local umpire will be hired for the final two games of the series, and Cricks and Fullwood will be required to perform extra work behind home plate. No matter. One of their own has been called to the major leagues. For one day, this difficult life they have chosen, a life without promises or guarantees, seems worth it.

There are 225 umpires toiling in the minor leagues, from rookie ball to Triple-A. But there are only 68 jobs available at the big league level.

"No one has ever figured it out," Spagnardi says, "but I'd say the chances of going to the majors and sticking is about 1 percent."

The average ump may need seven to 10 years in the minors before getting a shot in The Show. That's twice as long as it takes the average ballplayer.

It's an endless summer when you're a minor league umpire: no in-season vacations, one hotel after another, few chances to see family members and modest salaries.

"Everyone is chasing the same dream," Spagnardi says. "Everyone wants to get to the majors."

Spagnardi is in his eighth season umpiring and his third at Triple-A. He was called up a few times last season, and on this night learns he'll work two games in Cincinnati and three in Denver.

"My mom and dad were the first ones I called," he says. "I had several family members who were planning to drive up from North Carolina to Scranton to see me later in the week. I had to call and cancel their plans."

Last year, Spagnardi's family drove 15 hours to watch him work in Detroit.

"They got to see the dream in person," he says. "To see their son and brother walk out onto a major league stadium in full uniform — it was awesome."

Not everyone is as fortunate as Spagnardi.

Cricks is in his seventh year as an umpire and his first at Triple-A. Fullwood is an eighth-year ump in his second season at Triple-A. Both have yet to reach the Promised Land.

"It's our dream, obviously," Fullwood says. "It's the dream of every umpire."

And that's the problem. Everyone wants in, and big league umpires stick around for decades. "Many guys work for 20, 30 years," says Marty Springstead, a former American League umpire whose job now is grading umpires around the country for The Professional Baseball Umpire Corporation, which oversees all professional baseball umpires. "It's a great job with a lot of perks."

Just as players are graded by managers after every game, so too are umps.

Their grades come from league presidents and baseball executives (usually former umps) who travel around the country and file reports.

People who want to become professional umpires can do so by attending one of two training schools for a five-week course during the off-season: the Jim Evans Academy of Professional Umpiring in Kissimmee, Florida, or the Harry Wendelstedt School for Umpires in Ormond Beach, Florida, both named after former veteran umps.

About 300 aspiring umpires apply each year at the two schools. The best are eventually funneled into the minor league system.

Umpires become umpires for different reasons. Spagnardi's older brother gave it a shot and ultimately quit, but Darren's fire was lit. Fullwood, a high school math teacher in Hampton, Virginia, in the offseason, did it to supplement his income. And Cricks loved the sport so much he decided to find a way to stay close to it. "I gave umpiring a try and fell in love with it," he says.

The differences between the life of a big-league ump and one in the minors are enormous.

Major-league umpires receive five weeks of vacation each season. Some even take them as late as August. Minor league umps get no in-season vacation.

We might get a day off in Louisville or someplace," Spagnardi says. "What good does that do me when I live in Lexington, North Carolina?"

Absence does not make the heart grow fonder in this business. Spagnardi is divorced, and his crewmates have never been married.

"We were heading in that direction anyway," Spagnardi says of his marriage, "but this job certainly didn't help matters."

He estimates that at least 50 percent of the umpires he knows are divorced.

"It's not a good job if you want to be married and raise a family," he says. "You're pretty much on the road for five months straight."

Big-league umps are paid anywhere from $84,000 (for rookies) to $340,000 (for veterans with 25-plus years' service). They fly first class to some of the nation's top cities with a per diem of $320.

Triple-A umpires receive a salary in the range of $2,500 to $3,400 per month, with a per diem of $25. Their hotel rooms and rental cars are paid for by the host team, and they receive a meal in their locker room. Umpires in rookie ball make as little as $1,800 per month. Many umps supplement their income by working winter ball in places like Venezuela and Puerto Rico. Cricks is an instructor for the Wendelstedt school.

"The rule book is in the mind," he says. "The (winter) job doesn't pay much, but it gives me a chance to stay sharp."

Umpiring crews are composed of three or four men, depending on big league needs, and the crews are chosen before each season.

"I've been lucky," Spagnardi says. "I've gotten along with all of my crewmates over the years. But there are others who aren't as lucky.

"Some crews have personality conflicts, and it makes for a real long season when you have to spend so much time together in cars and hotels."

Umpires know when crewmates blow calls, but there is a code of conduct that each follows:

Don't speak unless spoken to. "You never want to show up another ump," Fullwood says. "There are ways to get his attention if you know he's blown one. Last year, we had a signal. If one of us took our hat off or rubbed our head, it meant, 'Come talk to me.'"

The three umpires in this crew pause when asked whether they read the daily newspaper accounts of the games they work. Finally, Fullwood says, "I don't."

Why not?

"How many times do you read where an umpire had a good game?" he says. "You only read about controversial calls and stuff like that."

He's right, of course. Umpires are said to have their best games when no one notices their work.

You might think an umpire loves working behind home plate, calling the balls and strikes and making huge decisions on plays at the plate.

In most cases, you would be wrong.

"It's not the icing on the cake," Fullwood says. "It's the green beans."

Indeed, working the plate takes a toll on an umpire's concentration.

The three-man crews in the minors (and four-man crews in the majors) rotate around the bags, but there are times when an umpire is forced to work the plate multiple times in a given homestand. "It's grinding," Spagnardi says.

Still, ask any ump to name his dream scenario and he'll list the same one: Game 7, World Series, working behind the plate.

"That would be the ultimate," Fullwood says.

An umpire must make split-second decisions on more than 200 pitches each game, and often deal with players and managers who can't understand how anyone could call that inside fastball a strike. He doesn't sit down between innings, whether it's 40 degrees or 90, and he's not supposed to let personal feelings dictate his calls.

"The rule you have to follow is, 'Be your own person,'" Spagnardi says. "You can't hide who you are. Be true, and be honest."

Spagnardi says there is a quick way to earn an ejection, however.

"Anytime you throw 'you' into it, I'm likely to run you," he says. "If you say, 'You blew that call' or 'You are a terrible ump,' you're probably gone. Don't make it personal."

In another era, umpires who didn't see the writing on the wall would toil in the minors for years, decades.

These days, there is a retention system. Umpires not promoted to the next level within two years are released. Once they reach Triple-A, they have three years to make the majors — unless the powers that be at Major League Baseball decide to keep them around.

Mike VanVleet is in his sixth year at Triple-A. He has seen some big league action and keeps churning away.

It's a tough life, a lonely life, one that ends with fulfillment for only a fraction of those who put in the time.

"We're all chasing the same dream," Cricks says, "and we're the only friends we have in baseball."

CHRIS COLABELLO: FIELD OF DREAMS

Published June 25, 2013

First baseman Chris Colabello spent seven long seasons toiling in an independent baseball league and another year playing Double-A ball. But in 2013, his perseverance paid off. Colabello was named International League MVP after a sensational year for the Rochester Red Wings. More importantly, he earned his first trip to the major leagues.

CHRIS COLABELLO HAS HIS BAGS PACKED. HIS BASEBALL CAREER may be over. It is spring 2005, and the Worcester Tornadoes of the independent Can-Am League are releasing the first baseman. They've strung him along for 10 days and now tell him there's no place on the roster.

Through those days in limbo, Colabello has shown up for workouts and played as if it were Game 7 of the World Series. First to arrive, last to leave. On this final night, he sticks around to watch the game and say his goodbyes in the clubhouse. That's when Tornadoes manager Rich Gedman sees him — and reprieves him. "I'll see you at batting practice tomorrow," the former Boston Red Sox catcher says. "The way you worked this week, when you didn't even have a roster spot, is what I like about you. Don't ever change."

It's a lesson Colabello took to heart, through one disappointment after another. Seven years thriving in independent ball, with a career average of .317, 86 total homers and 420 runs batted in.

Cut from the Italian World Baseball Classic team in 2006. Released after a tryout with the Detroit Tigers in spring training that same year.

But Colabello's perseverance is as long as his name. A year ago, he finally landed in organized baseball. And this year, after a fast start with the Triple-A Rochester Red Wings, he earned a big league call-up to the Minnesota Twins.

"It's all awesome," says Colabello, now back with the Wings. "But at the end of the day it's baseball, whether it's Target Field (in Minneapolis), Frontier Field or New Britain Stadium. The bells and whistles are a lot better in the majors, but the more I focus on them the less I'm capable of being myself."

There have been 38 players in history who started in independent ball and reached the majors. None played longer in an independent league – which is not part of organized baseball - than Colabello. He's making history while making his story an inspiration to those around him. "It's a story that amazes us," Wings second baseman Eric Farris says. "He stuck it out for so long. Not many guys could do that and then get a chance and make the most of it. He inspires us."

Colabello isn't just the best player on the team. He might be the most popular.

"He brings it all," Farris says. "He's one of those guys everyone wants to be around."

Colabello's childhood was a tale of two cities: Milford, Massachusetts, a city of 53,000 whose No. 3 employer is Subway; and Rimini, Italy, one of the most famous seaside resorts in Europe, with an endless sandy beach on the Adriatic Sea. His dad, Lou, was a left-handed pitcher who led the University of Massachusetts to the 1969 College World Series and then played pro ball in Italy. He pitched for Rimini from 1977 to 1984, finishing with a 94-25 record and a 2.99 earned-run average. More importantly, he met his future wife, Italian-born Silvana, over there.

In Lou's final season, he pitched for the Italian National Team against Team USA in the 1984 Olympics at Dodger Stadium. Chris, an only child, was 1 at the time.

The family continued to divide their time between Italy and the United States before finally settling in Massachusetts as Chris neared junior high. He enjoyed a strong varsity career at Milford High — he was also on the golf team — but didn't attract any Division I interest until he already had committed to nearby Division III Assumption College. He was an all-conference selection his final three seasons but was not selected in the baseball draft.

Rochester Red Wings first baseman Chris Colabello high-fives manager Gene Glynn as he rounds third base after hitting a home run against Scranton/ Wilkes-Barre RailRiders in 2013 at Frontier Field. Photographer: Kris Murante

"Around the 48th round my senior year, I get a phone call from my college coach," Colabello recounts. "He was close friends with one of the Tornadoes assistants, and they asked me to try out."

This was Worcester's first year as a pro team. Colabello didn't even know what independent ball was. He worked out for Gedman and was signed, but his career was over almost before it started. He had enjoyed just eight at-bats when team officials told him he would be released for the weekend while the Tornadoes signed an extra catcher. A catcher on their roster was having visa issues, and the team was headed to Quebec.

Ten days later, the Tornadoes told Colabello they'd found someone else. And that was also when Gedman came to his rescue.

"He saved me many times," Colabello says. "I was angry when

I didn't get drafted. I didn't understand. But Rich said to me, 'The game owes you nothing. What makes you so special?' He was right. I stopped feeling like baseball owed me something and started feeling like I owed everything to the game."

Colabello made just $750 a month that first year — "$332 after taxes" — and lived with his parents. The per diem was $18. He remembers a magazine in Worcester plastering his photo and salary on the cover.

"I said, 'Nobody's gonna be impressed by that!'" he says with a laugh. Colabello's salary gradually increased to the point where he was making $2,200 a month his seventh and final year in independent ball. By comparison, major league rookies make $2,722 *per day*.

To supplement his income during those rough years, he helped Gedman conduct baseball clinics in the offseason. All the while, he tried to get into organized baseball. Then, in 2007, the rebuilding Tornadoes traded him to rival Nashua at midseason. "I was shocked," he says. "I looked at Rich, and he said, 'This might be the best thing to happen to you.' And he was right. I'd been there so long. I no longer had to be *the* guy who carried everyone in the clubhouse, the guy who had to explain why we didn't get paid on time or didn't have a clubhouse spread after a game."

Nashua won the championship that year, managed by another former Boston Red Sox star — Butch Hobson. Then Colabello became a free agent and re-signed with Worcester out of respect to Gedman.

Gedman, now the hitting coach for the Double-A Portland Sea Dogs, said the one thing that quickly became apparent about Colabello was his ability to hit .300.

"Most guys, regardless of what league they play in, that number is magic," Gedman says. "Some guys can't get there. Chris did it for seven years straight, and that's the sign of a very good hitter no matter what league they play in. But I don't know if anyone could have projected he'd make it to the big leagues."

Every year after the season ended, a few big league teams would send Colabello a letter asking him to fly there for a tryout (at his expense). And he did it.

"But at some point, I realized the tryout thing wasn't working for me," he says. "I finally told teams, 'What do you need to see me do? By now, my numbers speak for themselves. I'm not going to run the 60 faster than someone else. I might not throw it across the infield better than someone else or take BP better. You need to watch me play. You need to give me spring training.'"

In 2011, *Baseball America* magazine named him its Independent Leagues Player of the Year after he hit .348 with 20 homers and 79 RBI for Worcester. And finally — finally! — someone noticed. The Twins signed him and sent him to their Double-A club in New Britain, Connecticut, where he hit .284 with 19 homers and a franchise-record 98 RBI.

This spring, Colabello was invited to big-league camp and found his locker sandwiched between those of Twins stars (and former American League MVPs) Joe Mauer and Justin Morneau.

"I thought it was a joke," he says.

His spring with the Twins was interrupted by the World Baseball Classic. Chris played for Team Italy — just like his dad — and was one of the tournament's breakout stars. He went 4-for-5 with a homer and four RBI at Chase Field in Phoenix against Canada. And he hit a three-run homer in Miami against the eventual champion, the Dominican Republic.

Colabello was assigned to Rochester, a 29-year-old Triple-A rookie. And by May 22, when he was hitting .358 with an International League high of 12 homers, he was teammates with Mauer and Morneau for real. Colabello was playing cards with teammates on a bus traveling home from Allentown, Pennsylvania, in the early morning hours, when he saw Wings manager Gene Glynn walking toward him.

"Hey, I've got some news," Glynn said. "You're going to the big leagues."

Colabello was speechless. "All I could say was, 'What?'" he says with a laugh. "And then there were a ton of emotions: tears, laughter, joy."

Glynn was thrilled for his star.

"He's a leader who loves the game and plays it like it's his last," Glynn says. "When you have guys with that kind of heart and spirit for this game, it spreads."

An hour later, a woman driving a car slammed into the bus, grinding the trip home to a temporary halt. One problem: Colabello had to catch a 6 a.m. flight to Atlanta for a day game.

"Everybody was like, 'Dude, you need to get back,'" he says. "And I'm like, 'How am I going to get back?'"

He made it in time to catch his flight, slept 30 minutes on the plane and found himself in the starting lineup. With one out in the second inning, he slammed the first pitch he saw to right field.

"I thought it was a double," he says, "but (Braves outfielder) Jason Heyward had other ideas."

Colabello would pick up his first big league hit three days later — a single off Doug Fister in Detroit — with his parents and longtime girlfriend Alison Connor in the stands. The popular rookie was given the game ball by Twins manager Ron Gardenhire, and every teammate shook his hand. His proud parents took the ball, a symbol of resilience, home to Massachusetts.

"It was a long wait for a guy who has persevered through a lot," Gardenhire told reporters. "A lot of people told him it wouldn't work out for him, but he never quit and he got his opportunity and he got his hit."

Colabello would gain a bit of notoriety on May 29 when he wore the wrong jersey — he donned the TWINS uniform and his teammates wore MINNESOTA — while pinch-hitting in Milwaukee. The uniforms are identical except for the script across the front, but the story became fodder for tweeters and bloggers.

"I thought it was a prank at first," he says. "But I don't think they'd do that to me. The clubby puts the jerseys in our locker facing out, and I saw the Twins one. I didn't know there were two different ones, to be honest."

He got to wear two jerseys plenty over the following two weeks during a repeated shuffle between Minneapolis and Rochester.

"I got to spend a lot of time in airports," he says. "But that's OK. It's all great."

If you think he's satisfied now that he's "made it," you don't know Chris Colabello.

"My goal was never just to get to the major leagues," he says. "I want to stay there and have a long career."

Gedman used to tell him: "It's the same game in the minors and majors, Chris. Just don't pay attention to the names on the backs of the jerseys." But after year after year of low pay and small rewards, it's hard not to pay attention to the name on the front of Colabello's jersey. It says RED WINGS now, but it said TWINS before and almost certainly will again. And when he thinks about it, Colabello allows himself a chance to smile.

"It's pretty awesome," he says. "It's pretty great."

UNIVERSITY PREP: SLAM-DUNKING STEREOTYPES

Published January 1, 2013

The Rochester, New York City School District has taken its hits over the years. Low attendance. Even lower graduation rates. Then along comes University Prep, a charter school with near-100-percent attendance, good grades—and a championship basketball team.

JOE MUNNO RETIRED IN 2008 AFTER 37 YEARS IN THE Rochester School District as a teacher, coach and principal. But he soon wondered if he had left too soon.

"Did I accomplish enough?" the Greece resident wondered. "And the answer was 'no.'"

So three years ago the 63-year-old Munno opened a charter school for boys and became principal. The result was University Preparatory Charter School for Young Men — UPrep for short — a boys-only school that is shattering cultural stereotypes while making sports history.

The basketball team consists only of eighth, ninth and 10th-graders — there is no junior or senior class — but won the Section V Class D1 title and reached the state semifinals before losing to Martin Luther King of Section I in Glens Falls. The Griffins ended the season 19-4.

UPrep opened with seventh- and eighth-graders and has added a class every year. A junior class will be formed this fall, and a senior class in 2014. It is one of seven charter schools in Rochester, but the only one in western New York with an all-male enrollment. And that's by design.

"Boys do better when females aren't around," said Munno, a Rochester native who insists that students wear dress shirts and ties and homework must be completed before practice or games. Evening and weekend study sessions are held for struggling students.

"We like the structure because we're all one big family," says basketball star Marique Simkin, who became the first eighth-grader selected MVP of a Section V tournament two weeks ago.

"I'm happy I made history," he says. "But I plan on winning states every year with this team."

UPrep is for boys who live in the city of Rochester. According to the most recently available state report card (2010-11), 86 percent of UPrep students were living in poverty (free or reduced lunch) and 87 percent were black or Hispanic. The school is funded by the state. As in city schools, Munno receives $12,800 per student. There are 306 students in grades 7-10, and a waiting list for each class. All but two of the current students live in the city. The other two live in Greece and Gates but were city residents when they initially enrolled. "And we weren't about to tell them they had to leave," says Munno, whose building includes 32 teachers and 20 staffers.

There is no tuition fee but also no guarantee of enrollment.

"By April 1, if there are more than 75 applicants (for each class), we hold a lottery," Munno says. "We pull names. The first 75 get in. The rest go on a waiting list."

UPrep's motto is "changing a culture for eight hours a day." Last semester, 114 students made the honor roll and were celebrated at a school assembly. Munno demands parents show up for such occasions.

"If they don't, I'll call and say, 'You embarrassed your son by not being here,'" he says.

The ceremony was attended by 400 people and was followed by a spaghetti and meatball dinner.

UPrep freshman Krasny Gonzalez says he was "excited" when he heard about the new school three years ago and still is.

"I love the structure because it makes everyone equal," he said. "No one can make fun of each other."

Education means everything to Munno. A former head football coach at Marshall High in Rochester, he remembers telling three players years ago that if they graduated from college he would find jobs for them. Today, Brenton Brady is UPrep's school counselor, Chaz Bruce is a fine arts teacher and Terrell Cunningham

UPrep basketball coach Raheem Miller speaks to his team after a 2012 practice. Photographer: Marie De Jesus

is in charge of student security. UPrep's athletic director is Dick Cerone, longtime Section V football chairman. The athletic programs include soccer, football, basketball, boxing (rare for varsity), baseball and track. Lacrosse, a sport not associated with many urban schools, starts in April at the modified level. "That's what it's all about," head coach Arkee Allen says. "Giving them something they've never done before."

Munno believes that if you make school fun, kids will attend. That's why UPrep has book-reading goals and chooses a "writer of the month" for each class, posting that student's photo on hallway walls. It's why students script and produce their own musical videos, Gangnam style. And it's why UPrep is the only urban school in Monroe County that participates in Master Minds (think the old College Bowl). "We won our first match last week against East Rochester, too," Munno says proudly.

Each Thursday, he takes 20 students to a farm in Pittsford. The boys started out cleaning the stables, then moved on to taking care of the horses. Now they ride them.

"You have to create things that bring them to school," says Munno, adding that his daily attendance is 98 percent.

UPrep already has outgrown its antiquated home, which was once an all-boys military school and later a co-ed K-through-6 building. Munno purchased it from the Sisters of St. Joseph's for $400,000. Next week, he'll make a formal purchase offer on the old Aberdeen Nursing Home at the corner of Seneca Parkway and Lake Avenue. If it's approved, a three-year, $2 million project will soon begin that will house the entire school. Munno also plans to construct a gym.

"That's my final chapter," he says.

The current gym includes just two baskets, and is so small that athletes in other sports stretch in academic hallways. UPrep did not host any basketball games this year, playing "home games" at St. John Fisher, Roberts Wesleyan, Wilson Magnet and Gates Chili. And yet, the blue-and-gold Griffins are two wins from a state championship despite fielding only modified (seventh- and eighth-grade) and freshman teams last year.

Head coach Raheem Miller, who played football at Michigan State in the 1990s, says times have changed.

"City kids today don't have the motivation for sports we had," he says. "Sports isn't enough to get them to go to school."

Miller coached varsity football to a 1-9 record last fall. The roster included just 19 players, with an eighth-grader (Simkin) at quarterback and a 5-foot-3 freshman (basketball star Brandon Hunt) at tailback. Hunt didn't come to UPrep by choice. He thought he'd be headed to nearby East High, a school with a tradition of athletic excellence.

"My parents told me I was coming," he said. "(My mom) said she wanted me to be successful in life. So I said I'd go. Now I love it. The teachers care about you, the coaches care about you. They keep you up whenever you're down."

Munno says he has been re-energized by UPrep, "even though my wife thinks I'm nuts." And he still has big plans before he leaves.

"I want a hockey team," he says. "And I want a band."

SETH JOHNSTON:
YOU'RE NEVER TOO OLD

Published February 13, 2007

Seth Johnston took a 10-year break from basketball, but in 2007 he returned at age 29 to join the Brockport Golden Eagles college team.

TEN YEARS AGO, FRESHMAN FORWARD SETH JOHNSTON WAS PLAY-ing junior varsity basketball for Nazareth College in Pittsford, New York. He was also having one heck of a time in the classroom.

"Playing basketball was great, because I had always dreamed of playing college ball," he said. "But things weren't working out academically. I didn't have my head on too straight. Too much freedom, I guess."

Long story short: Johnston dropped out of Nazareth after one year, worked a series of jobs for the next six, resumed his studies at nearby Monroe Community College and wound up at SUNY Brockport, where he's playing varsity ball for the high-flying Golden Eagles. He's married, a homeowner ... and having the time of his life.

"The guys have been awesome here," he said. "They've been so supportive. I thought the opposing fans would razz me, but they don't list ages on the roster and I don't look 20. Maybe now they will."

What's to razz? The 6-foot-4, 200-pound Johnston has been a key reserve for the Eagles, averaging 5.2 points in about 10 minutes of action per game. The stats say he has eight assists, but that doesn't count the numerous ones he has dished out on the bench or off the court to his younger teammates.

"He motivates us and keeps us going," said Brockport junior swingman Brandon Williams, who befriended Johnston two years ago. "He's my best friend, like a brother, and he tries real hard out there."

Johnston finds it easy to aid his teammates. "I can see the potential pitfalls because I've been there," he says. "If I think they're going down the wrong road, I keep them focused on what the prize is."

Johnston grew up in Marion, a small town in Wayne County, New York, and played three years of varsity basketball. He averaged 20 points and 10 rebounds his senior year, earning All-Greater Rochester honorable mention as the Black Knights won the Section V Class CC title. He was recruited that winter by a young Nazareth assistant named Nelson Whitmore — now Brockport's head coach — and decided to attend Nazareth. Part of his financial aid was contingent on maintaining a specific GPA; when he didn't, he left after one year rather than spend more money on school. He spent the next several years in a variety of jobs, from delivering for Clover Home Leisure Centers and prefabricating hotel molds for hotel operator E.J. Del Monte, to flipping pizzas and working construction on apartment complexes.

In 2003, he decided to return to college and enrolled at MCC. "My mom and dad always knew I had the potential to do good things, to go to school and do well," he said, "but it was something I had to figure out for myself."

He talked with MCC coach Jerry Burns about trying out but decided to focus on his studies. He was at MCC for two years before continuing his education at Brockport as a physical education major in 2005.

Johnston had never stopped loving, or playing, basketball. He stayed in shape by playing in men's leagues three nights a week, and the desire to play college ball still burned inside him. But that first year at Brockport, he had far too many eggs in the basket to fit in a basketball.

Johnston and his wife, Jessica, were married 3½ years ago and have a house in Greece.

"No children yet, but we're planning on it," said Johnston. He also works in developmental aid at the Monroe Developmental Center, where he helps five adults in a group home. He makes dinner, passes out medications, does laundry and takes the group out for activities.

Work, family and school kept Johnston busy that first year at Brockport. He stayed in contact with Whitmore, and met many of his current teammates at open gyms. They all urged him to give basketball another shot.

Jessica, an accountant for Blue Choice, also gave her blessing. "That was huge," Johnston said. "She's so supportive of me."

"Coach Whitmore and I figured out I only had two semesters of eligibility left. I decided I didn't want to get further on in my life and look back with regrets."

He not only made the team, he made the team much better.

"He's a great shooter who is strong and mature," Whitmore said. "He's only 6-4, but he gives us a strong physical presence on the boards."

Whitmore didn't recognize Johnston when the aspiring player came to his office last fall, but he quickly warmed to the idea of having a veteran on the team.

"I knew he could play out of high school," said Whitmore, who is only eight years older than Johnston. "At 40 pounds heavier, I figured he would be a better version 10 years later."

Johnston, who was a teammate of Brockport assistant Greg Dunne at Nazareth, is thrilled that he gave it the old college try. He's on track to graduate in May 2008, and the aspiring teacher and coach has recorded grade point averages of 3.5 and 3.3 in the past two semesters.

"I'm so happy for the second chance, at school and basketball," Johnston said. "When I was at Nazareth, I didn't realize the opportunity I had in front of me."

His hectic schedule means late nights and early mornings, but it's worth it when the game ends and he's greeted with a hug and kiss from Jessica.

"To have this be my last shot at playing college basketball and be on a team so focused and having so much success, it makes it that much more special," he says. "The whole thing is pretty surreal at times."

MIKE NEER: BUILDING A LEGACY

Published February 23, 2001

*I visited University of Rochester men's basketball coach Mike Neer
at his office in 2001 for what was supposed to be a one-hour interview.
I ended up staying three hours. The man is one of the more
fascinating and articulate coaches in Rochester history.*

IT'S 1964, AND MIKE NEER IS WRITING WHAT AMOUNTS TO A
letter of resignation from the varsity basketball team at St. Stephen's
Episcopal School for Boys in Alexandria, Virginia.

Dear Coach, I quit. No one is going to talk to me like that.

Neer was a skinny junior whose opponent had just turned him
inside out on the court that day. Neer's coach, Sleepy Thompson,
questioned his toughness after the game.

"It felt like a real affront," Neer recalls. "I'd never been challenged like that."

Neer couldn't sleep that night. He wrote several versions of his
farewell address, but all of them found their way to his wastepaper
basket. For that, scores of University of Rochester players are grateful. Neer not only returned the next day, he followed in Thompson's
coaching footsteps.

For the past 25 years, Neer has roamed the UR sidelines, racking
up a school-record 378 victories and winning a national championship in 1990. He likes to quip that he is also the school's all-time los-
ingest coach with 267 losses.

"If you were trying to put food on the table, I don't think you'd
be wanting to coach against Mike every night," says St. John Fisher
coach Bob Ward. "He's usually going to have a very disciplined,
cerebral team that executes. Heaven help you if he gets a couple of
post players, because then he's going to kill you."

Neer was born in Boston but grew up in Alexandria. There were only 45 boys in Neer's class at St. Stephen's, so Thompson found a way for the skinny kid to play football.

"I was tight end, goal post, down marker, punter, place kicker — anything that involved as little contact as possible," he says.

Neer went on to play basketball at Washington & Lee University in Lexington, Virginia, where he earned All-Virginia Small College honors and graduated with a degree in sociology. He was invited to a few postseason All-Star tournaments after college, and — surprise, surprise — was drafted in the 15th round in 1970 by the NBA's Cincinnati Royals, whose roots, ironically, were in Rochester.

"Looking back, I was just an extra body in camp," says Neer, who was ultimately cut. "I also was drafted by the United States government (during the Vietnam War). And Uncle Sam had a no-cut contract."

Neer had thought he was exempt from service because he stood 6-foot-7, and the maximum height was 6-6.

"I was Joe College," he says. "I was too tall."

But during his physical, he was told that the height limit had been raised to 6-8.

"I was whistling all the way down on the bus," he says. "I wasn't whistling on the way back."

Neer was negotiating with an Italian pro team at the time, and the club even offered to make him an Italian citizen.

"You have a draft, too," Neer told team officials. "I've seen your record. The last battle you won was in 1938 against Ethiopia. I'll take my chances with Uncle Sam."

Neer was waiting for boot camp to begin when an acquaintance — who also happened to be an admiral in the Navy — invited him over to talk about staying involved in basketball while in the service.

Neer's father, Casper, was a Navy lieutenant junior grade during World War II before later becoming an architect. Neer called the Navy coach and landed a job interview 45 minutes away in Annapolis.

"I ran down the stairs, had my sister trim my hair 'cause I looked like a child from the '70s, and did the interview," he recalls. "And I got the job."

Neer coached the Navy plebe (freshman) team from 1972-76, recording a 41-18 record. One of his wins was over a young coach named Mike Krzyzewski who was coaching the West Point Prep School before beginning his legendary career at Duke.

"They came in undefeated and we beat them," Neer recalls, "but he got me a few times."

In 1976, Neer learned that the University of Rochester was looking for a coach following the retirement of Lyle Brown after 19 years.

"We had played Rochester in one of my early years, and I had scouted them at Hartwick," he says. "I knew it was a good private school. It fit a profile I could identify with."

The feeling was mutual. In April 1976, at age 27, Neer was hired by then-UR athletic director Dave Ocorr.

"He emphasized discipline and defense," Ocorr says. "He was a cerebral coach, like Pete Carril at Princeton."

John Mattioli, a sophomore forward on Neer's first team, said nobody expected Neer to stick around UR.

"The rumors were flying that Jim Boeheim had got the job, but then he went to Syracuse," says Mattioli, who runs an industrial equipment sales company in Atlanta with former UR teammate Jim Klimschot. "We figured Mike was big time because he came from Navy. We thought, 'He's going to make his mark here and then take off.'"

Ocorr says he never offered the job to Boeheim, then an assistant at Syracuse.

"I think he might have been frustrated recruiting the talent we were used to," Ocorr says.

Neer was only five years older than the seniors but left no doubt about who was in charge.

"He was young and full of you-know-what and vinegar," Mattioli says. "He was tough. He wasn't afraid of a confrontation if that's what he thought would motivate you.

"He'd try to call out the toughness in you."

Just as Sleepy Thompson had done to Neer years before.

Success was not automatic. UR went 22-45 in Neer's first three seasons. But the Yellowjackets weren't exactly playing the YMCA junior varsity. On December 10, 1977, UR ventured into Chapel Hill, North Carolina, to take on Dean Smith's dominant North Carolina Tar Heels.

UNC scored the game's first 22 points and opened the second half with a 22-2 run. Final score: 101-43.

"I knew we were in trouble when the kids were asking (UNC star) Phil Ford for his autograph before the game," Neer says.

Since 1987, Neer has recorded only three losing seasons. The dream year was 1989-90. Led by a sophomore center named Chris Fite, UR rolled to a 27-5 record and the program's first NCAA Division III title, beating DePauw (Indiana) 43-42 in the championship game.

"We knew we had a good team, but I don't think anyone anticipated what would happen," says McQuaid graduate John Kelly, the point guard on that championship team.

"Coach was just a great tactician that year. Every pass meant something, and every possession meant something."

Neer is an intense coach, yet he has received only seven technicals in his 25 years. Kelly says Neer can pick his spots.

"He expected a lot out of us but he knew when to be tough on us and when not. Before the championship game, he told us, 'I have nothing to say. You know what you have to do. We're ready. Let's go do it.'"

The National Association of Basketball Coaches named Neer its Division III Coach of the Year in 1990. He was also offered the coaching job at Columbia University. It meant a return to Division I, twice the money and a chance to shine in New York City.

Neer turned it down.

"I don't need that Ivy League label," he says. "Here, I'm 10 minutes from Cobbs Hill to school and I coach basically the same kids I'd have at Columbia. There, I might have to live in Jersey or Rockland County and fight through the darn George Washington Bridge every day."

Two years after winning it all, Rochester returned to the national championship. This time, the Yellowjackets fell 61-48 to Calvin, Michigan. That sadness was nothing compared to the next day, when Neer learned Sleepy Thompson had passed away.

"He was somebody who caught you at an age where you're a work in progress," says Neer, who was a pallbearer at Thompson's funeral. "He was a great man."

Michael Coleman, who played on UR's championship club and later was a Yellowjackets assistant, says Neer has mellowed through the years.

"The kids on this year's team think he's tough," Coleman says, "but he was harder on us. And yet after we won the championship, there were tears in his eyes. He loved that team."

Last December, members of the 1990 championship team reunited at the renovated UR Palestra. Neer surprised them with a gift: pieces of the former Palestra floor, with personal inscriptions to each player.

Mike Neer is the son of an architect, and during road trips he marvels at Frank Lloyd Wright's work in Chicago, and the Gateway Arch in St. Louis.

"I'll quiz the team on different buildings," he says. "It's in my blood, because of my dad."

Casper Neer passed away in 1981. Neer once thought he wanted to follow in his dad's footsteps. And in a way he has.

He has built a legacy.

ED AND MARY BLASKO:
A FATHER-DAUGHTER HOME RUN

Published July 2, 2004

*There are fans, there are super fans and then there are the Blaskos of
Pittsford, New York. Ed and his daughter Mary have been regulars at
Rochester Red Wings baseball games since the mid-1980s,
and even see the team on the road.*

MARY BLASKO WAS THRILLED WHEN SHE RECEIVED A SPECIAL
Christmas present from her father, Ed, in 1985: season tickets to
Rochester Red Wings games at Silver Stadium.

"I've always been a baseball fan," says Mary, who was 24 at the
time. "I thought it was a great gift."

Little did she know it would be the gift that kept on giving. And
giving. And giving. Now, 19 years later, the Blaskos have become as
familiar at Frontier Field as the trains that roll by. The Pittsford residents are not just season seat holders, they're ballpark staples. Mary
was named Season Seatholder of the Year in 1999, and Ed won it the
following year.

"Quite simply, Ed and Mary Blasko are two of the greatest Red
Wings fans I've met in the 61 years that I've been going to Red
Wings games," says season ticketholder Joe Paris of Greece. "Ask a
lot of the real good fans and the thing you get is this: It wouldn't be
the same without Mary and Ed around. Part of enjoying the game is
fans like them."

The Blaskos don't just attend games at Frontier; they also travel
to Syracuse and Buffalo – each about 80 miles away - 16 times each
summer to watch the Wings play. "They attend more games than
I do," says Red Wings general manager Dan Mason. "They're just
great, great fans who are extremely supportive of the team whether
they're winning or losing."

And, Mason adds, "They know everybody at the ballpark."

You will find them on the third-base side at Frontier, just behind the visitor's dugout. But don't look for them sitting together, because they don't. Mary sits in Section 123. Ed is next to Paris in Section 124 — when he's in his chair and not coaxing fans to participate in his nightly attendance derby (more on that later).

"When we started at Silver, we sat in the same section," Ed says. "But I wanted to sit a little higher and we couldn't get seats together (that high) when the team moved here. Since then, we've had one section separating us."

In truth, they are inseparable. Mary, who is single, is a homeowners adjuster for Allstate Insurance and lives with her parents. Her mom, Donna, attends games but not nearly as many as Ed and Mary.

The Blaskos rarely miss a Wings game if they can drive to it in under two hours. From April 23 through May 16, the Red Wings played every game either at Frontier Field or in Syracuse or Buffalo. The Blaskos attended all 23 of them.

"Ed and Mary are the definition of super fans," Mason says.

Each winter, they order four tickets to every Syracuse or Buffalo game involving the Wings ("We always bring someone along," Mary says) and sit in the same seats.

"I just love the atmosphere," Mary says. "I've even gone to Buffalo for postseason games when the Wings didn't make the playoffs."

The Blaskos missed two Frontier Field games last year, one to attend the graduation of Ed's twin granddaughters and another for a wedding.

"The reception was at the Crowne Plaza," Mary says. "We left and got in the car and we heard that the Wings were winning in a blowout and it was the ninth inning. So we just went back into the reception."

The Blaskos drive together each night — Ed takes the wheel of his 2001 Dodge Caravan on the way to games, and Mary drives home. They arrive at Frontier about 75 minutes before games. "Mary likes to get something to eat after work," Ed explains, "and I get together with a bunch of guys I know and we have a beer before the game starts."

Baseball has been a major part of their lives for decades, and not

Mary Blasko and her dad, Ed, are Red Wings season ticketholders. Here they are during a 2004 game at Frontier Field. Photographer: Max Schulte

just in Rochester. Ed's job as a high-ranking executive in Eastman Kodak's engineering services department kept his family on the move. Mary was born in Rochester but then lived in Los Angeles and Seattle, back to Rochester for a year, Chicago for 10 years and then back to Rochester in 1983.

"We loved going to Dodger games, and then to Wrigley Field (in Chicago)," Mary says. "Going to a Cubs game was the best. The fans in Chicago are like the fans here. It's like a family."

When the Blaskos returned to Rochester in 1983, Ed began attending Red Wings games alone or with Mary. He liked it so much, he decided to make it a family event for himself, Donna, Mary and son Ward.

Anyone who has attended a game at Frontier Field probably recognizes Ed. He's the bearded man who wears shorts all the time — "I bring a pair of pants in April just in case," he says — and has a wardrobe that seems to include every color in the rainbow.

"His wardrobe? Wow!" Mary says, laughing.

Ed owns more than 30 pairs of shorts: purple ones, green ones, black ones, red ones.

"I have matching socks and tops, or I mix and match and make them blend together," he says matter-of-factly.

Ed really turns heads on special occasions. This Easter, he wore bunny ears. On Flag Day, he was decked out in stars and stripes. On the Fourth of July, he's been known to dress like Uncle Sam.

"I love having fun and being sociable," he says. "I have no hesitation in teasing strangers. Anything that comes to mind, I'll say something foolish and make them laugh."

Mary sometimes gets into the act, like last month when she also showed her true colors (red, white and blue) on Flag Day. When the Wings held "Halloween in July" two years ago, Ed dressed as Mary and Mary dressed as Ed. The Blaskos passed out American flag stick-ons during the Flag Day game. They plan to hand out 75 pens next month.

"It will say something about the Red Wings and have 'Mary and Ed' with hugs and kisses," Ed says. Flag pins will be distributed on the Fourth of July. Bubble blowers are on the agenda later in the season.

Ed retired from Eastman Kodak after 35 years in 1992, but not before he earned his place in history. In 1982, he received a Scientific Engineering Award from the Academy of Motion Picture Arts and Sciences. That's right: Ed Blasko is an Oscar winner.

"*Recipient,*" he corrects. He and fellow Kodak employee Rod Ryan were presented the award by actor Lloyd Bridges, years after they developed the Prostar Microfilm Processor, which decreased the time it took studios to process special effects sequences.

These days, the prize that keeps Blasko motoring around Frontier Field is his attendance derby. The person whose guess about the number of paid attendees is closest to the reality wins the money.

"It started with just a few of us at Silver," Mary says. "Then we said, 'Let's each put in a quarter.' The pot was something like $3 or $5."

Not anymore. Ed saunters around the stadium during games with his paperwork and envelope, collecting quarters from anyone and everyone.

He often comes up with more than 100 entrees.

"Strangers come up to him and say, 'Can I get in on that?'" his daughter says. "Now the pot is up to $22 a night."

Even Rochester Bishop Matthew Clark has been known to chip in a quarter when he visits Frontier.

The Blaskos admit that the final five years of the Orioles' affiliation here (1998-2002) tested their love for the team and their nonstop attendance at games.

"It became disheartening," Mary says. "It was like 'Oh, we're going to the game again, and they're going to lose again.'"

The Blaskos used to be much more familiar with the players, especially at cozy Silver. Now, they tend to admire them from afar.

Both say the memories they have forged after almost two decades will last a lifetime.

"It's special to me," Mary says. "I have memories of sitting around in California with him and eating oranges out of a bowl. That's a nice childhood memory. But these 20 years and the memories we bring back and bring up in conversation, I won't be able to forget those at all."

Ed says he can't imagine a summer without his daughter accompanying him to the ballpark.

"It's so nice that we can enjoy each other's company," he says. "We really enjoy this, and we have so many great memories. We're buddies."

JONATHON LILLIS:
A SECOND CHANCE AT LIFE

Published December 25, 2010

This Christmas Day story told the inspiring tale of a young man who survived a near-fatal freak accident at home to become an elite aerial ski specialist.

JONATHON LILLIS DOESN'T REMEMBER ANYTHING ABOUT September 13, 2007. He doesn't recall waking up. Eating lunch. Babysitting his two younger brothers. Or nearly dying.

"The first thing I remember is waking up in the hospital a few days later," he says. "I felt normal. I was ready to leave. Then I tried to walk and nearly fell over. I had lost all of my strength."

Today, Lillis is a healthy, vibrant member of the U.S. Freestyle Ski Team, an aerial specialist who flips and somersaults with athletic grace.

He has an eye on the 2014 Winter Olympics in Sochi, Russia.

Three years ago, the mere act of walking would have been worthy of a gold medal celebration. Lillis was in big trouble.

It started out as a normal Thursday afternoon in Pittsford, a suburb east of Rochester, New York. With both parents gone, the three brothers were horsing around. Jonathon, then 13, was chasing 9-year-old Christopher and 7-year-old Michael when he slipped all the way down the stairs and caught the homemade hemp necklace he was wearing on the banister knob.

"It was one of those freak things," says his dad, Bernie. "He was wearing socks and slipped on the wooden stairs. In effect, he hung himself."

Their mother, Jamie, was driving home from her job as a first-grade teacher in the Rochester School District. Bernie had left the house minutes earlier and was sitting in his doctor's waiting room when Christopher called in a panic. He had found his brother hanging from the banister and had cut him down.

"Jon's not waking up!" he yelled into the phone.

Bernie instructed his son to get their neighbor, an emergency room doctor. While the family waited for an ambulance that seemingly took forever to arrive, the doctor extricated Jonathon's tongue from his throat, which allowed him to breathe.

Lillis was rushed to Golisano Children's Hospital at the University of Rochester Medical Center. No one knew how long he had stopped breathing, or how much damage there was. But the doctors had a plan. Four days earlier, Buffalo Bills tight end Kevin Everett had sustained a life-threatening spinal injury while attempting to tackle Denver Broncos kickoff return man Domenik Hixon.

Bills orthopedic surgeon Andrew Cappuccino had placed Everett in a hypothermic state to minimize swelling by running ice-cold saline through his system. Two days later, Everett voluntarily moved his arms and legs. He was up and walking three months later.

By an amazing coincidence, doctors at the Golisano pediatrics unit were talking the day of Lillis' injury about how effective the Everett treatment had been and how they would utilize that option if given the chance.

Hours later, Lillis was wheeled in and a similar hypothermic procedure was used. Lillis was put into a medically induced coma. A device known as the Arctic Sun Temperature Management System — in effect a vest filled with chilled water — was placed over Lillis' body. His temperature was allowed to drop to 92 degrees to prevent swelling to the brain, and it remained that way into the next day.

"The one organ that does not have regenerating powers is the brain," says Dr. Karen Powers, a pediatric critical care specialist at Golisano who was part of the team that treated Lillis. "If a reasonable amount of time passes where the brain has not been given adequate oxygen or blood flow, kids are at a high risk of a poor neurological outcome, including death."

Touching her eldest son, Jamie Lillis felt an eerie sensation.

"He was ice cold," she says. "Like he was dead."

Four days later, Lillis was awakened from his coma. But he was far from out of the woods.

"As a parent, you know you're in trouble when they're bringing in counselors to talk to you saying, 'He may not live. And if he does, he'll probably be a vegetable,'" Bernie says.

Powers says recent studies show that less than 40 percent of children survive after suffering a respiratory arrest outside of the hospital. Many more are permanently damaged.

Jamie couldn't even think about that.

"I had five million thoughts going through my head," she says. "One of them was, 'What will he do if he can't ski again?' Everything he did revolved around skiing."

To this day, Powers can't say with certainty if the hypothermia treatment saved Lillis' life. But she is amazed by how completely he recovered.

"For us, a great outcome is a kid walking and talking and being able to live independently," she says. "Maybe he has a bit of trouble with math, or he's a little clumsy. That's still an awesome outcome. For him to be able to become an elite athlete? That's an incredible story."

Before the accident, Lillis had been on the fast track to a fabulous skiing career. A skier by 6, he quickly grew bored on the slopes of Bristol Mountain and increasingly attracted to the more daring side of the sport. At 8, he switched to moguls (skiing on bumps, basically) and by 12 he attempted his first aerial jump and joined a freestyle team at Bristol, often competing against 18-year-old opponents across the East Coast.

"He was fearless," says his first coach, Johnny Kroetz, head coach of the Bristol Mountain Freestyle team. "He'd try one thing, and before he even mastered it he'd want to take it to the next level."

The 5-foot-6, 135-pound Lillis eventually focused solely on aerials, and trained for parts of two years with the Elite Aerial Team in Lake Placid.

"People were always coming up to us saying, 'He's really good. Do you know what he's doing on that hill?'" Jamie Lillis says. "When we saw Jon jump, you could see it. You'd be blind not to."

Aerial jumps are quite specific, and Lillis practiced endlessly on a trampoline in his family's back yard, or by landing in a deep pool. "It was all he could think about," his mom says.

The accident put everything on hold. Once it became clear Lillis would survive, the next challenge was mobility. First he moved his fingers and toes. Then he learned how to walk again. Three weeks after the injury, he walked out of the hospital.

As he was leaving, Lillis turned to one of the nurses and asked, "Ever see anybody as sick as I was?"

"None that lived," the nurse replied.

By January, just three months after the accident, Lillis was back doing his flips in the air. By March, his journey to the top of his sport would begin.

The family was sitting at home watching the national ski championships on TV.

"They were trying to drum up interest in aerials," Jamie Lillis says. "They said, 'If you're interested, send in a video.' So we put a video of Jon together and submitted it."

U.S. Freestyle officials invited Lillis for a trial at their headquarters in Lake Placid, and he ended up spending the summer there working out. He continued to train there throughout 2009 and into 2010. In October of 2010, at 16, he became the youngest member of the eight-person U.S. Freestyle men's "C team." The next youngest was 21.

Talk about a strong first impression: Lillis already has racked up five top-15 NorAm (North America) finishes and finished seventh at the U.S. Championships. Kroetz says Lillis' progression is incredible.

"They don't take you until you reach a certain level of progression," he says, "and that progression usually takes until you're 18 or 19.

"Coaches set out a plan. Do this by that date, and in five years you'll be here. Well, Jon was surpassing those goals and the coaches had to keep readjusting."

Kroetz isn't surprised that Lillis' climb to the top continued after his injury.

"Although the accident was traumatic and life-threatening, it's not like a car accident where bones are broken," Kroetz says. "Physically, he wasn't harmed, and by the grace of God he was able to keep his wits about him."

Lillis now calls Lake Placid his home. It's where he trains with the U.S. team and where he works toward his high school degree through Keystone University, an accredited online high school that offers 24-hour support from teachers. Basically, his parents buy classes and Jonathon has one year to complete them. He is just wrapping up his sophomore year.

"We're withholding his driver's license until he gets through sophomore year," his father says with a laugh.

It's not an easy process. Lillis teaches himself or asks teammates to help. It's a huge responsibility for a 16-year-old, but one he considers a necessity to pursue his dream of one day competing in the Olympics.

He comes home whenever possible. Sometimes for two weeks, sometimes two days.

"It took some getting used to, being away from my family," he says. "I miss my brothers and parents, but I'm used to being away."

His family rented a house in Lake Placid this past summer. Bernie was there all of July with his two other sons, and Jamie came up in August.

"As a mom, it's nerve-racking having him away," she says, "but he's very good at responding to us. He'll text or call every day."

If he doesn't, Mom finds inventive ways to get his attention.

"He always seems to reply to his brothers," she says. "So if he doesn't write back to me, I'll use one of their phones and text him."

Lillis says the most difficult challenge comes from within.

"It's a mental game," Jon says. "You get tired. Sometimes the body doesn't want to keep going, and sometimes the mind doesn't."

Lillis is sponsored by List2Move, a real estate company, but is hoping to garner more sponsors as his career progresses.

He doesn't remember his accident, but it has changed him dramatically.

"It's made me fearless," he says. "The worst thing that could possibly happen has already happened, and I'm fine."

The Olympic dream lives on.

"I wanted it before the accident," he says, "and now I want it so much more."

Jonathon Lillis doesn't remember anything about September 13, 2007. But he knows he was given a second chance at life — and he knows one more thing.

"I plan to make the most of it," he says.

SEAN BURROUGHS:
'LUCKY TO BE ALIVE'

Published June 24, 2012

From Little League World Series hero to drug addict and then major-league player, Sean Burroughs has been a fascinating character to follow.

"Life is about experiencing everything you can. I don't know how my baseball career will go, but I know I want my life to be an adventure."
— Sean Burroughs in *Sports Illustrated*, 2002

IT'S FAIR TO SAY BURROUGHS' LIFE HAS BEEN AN ADVENTURE. How many people can say they've been an extra on hit TV shows as a child? A Little League World Series hero with his own bubble gum card at 11? A guest on David Letterman's show at 12? An Olympic gold medalist at 20? And how many can say they quit the job they loved at 26 and spent four years in a paranoid drug haze, alienating friends and family, sleeping in motels because of a fear that intruders would storm the house in Las Vegas, eating cheeseburgers out of a trash can one night and ordering steak in a restaurant the next?

"People say I should write a book," Burroughs says, sitting in the home dugout at Frontier Field hours before a recent game. "I'd have enough material. I've had a lot happen to me."

These days, the 31-year-old Burroughs is back in baseball and done with drugs. He began the season in the major leagues with the Minnesota Twins but is currently a corner infielder with the Triple-A Rochester Red Wings.

And one more thing:

"I'm lucky to be alive," he says.

Burroughs grew up in Long Beach, California, and it was a great life for a baseball prodigy whose dad, Jeff, won the 1974 American

Rochester Red Wings first baseman Sean Burroughs offers to carry catcher J.R. Towles' equipment after he made a catch in foul territory during a 2012 game against the Charlotte Knights at Frontier Field. Photographer: Adrian Kraus

League MVP Award with the Texas Rangers.

"You'd go to the beach for 3-4 hours, come home and eat a couple of pizzas and then spank the hell out of the team we played that night," he says.

Burroughs, then 5-foot-5 and 170 pounds, was a self-described happy-go-lucky "fat kid who ate cheeseburgers."

According to a 2003 *ESPN The Magazine* feature, Burroughs "dressed" one Halloween as a flasher, complete with trench coat and a salami safety-pinned to his zipper. He appeared in background roles on hit shows like *Knots Landing, Dallas* and *Saved by the Bell.* He was also one of the finest players in Little League World Series history. Jeff retired when Sean was just 5, but the two would still share some amazing baseball moments.

In 1992, Sean was chosen to pitch and play shortstop for the Long Beach Little League All-Stars, with Jeff serving as head coach. The team lost in the finals of the Little League World Series in Williamsport, Pennsylvania, but were declared champions when the Filipino team was disqualified for using ineligible players. The next year, Long Beach repeated as champions and the mop-topped Burroughs — nicknamed "Burly" — became a media sensation after he hit .562 and threw two 16-strikeout no-hitters.

He was the life of the party. At Williamsport, he hijacked a tournament golf cart and drove it around town. He pulled a fire alarm after midnight, bringing six Williamsport fire trucks to the hotel. Nine days later, he appeared on Letterman. He played catch with the host on a New York City street and brought down the house when he said he wanted to be a gynecologist if baseball didn't work out.

"I think my buddy's dad was one, and I was a smartass," he says. "People still talk about it."

Burroughs went on to star at Wilson High, his dad's alma mater, and hit .528 with 7 home runs and 38 RBI in 29 games his senior year. He graduated with a 3.85 grade point average and a terrific 1,200 on the SATs. Southern Cal, a legendary college program, offered him a full ride. But the San Diego Padres offered him a $2.1 million signing bonus after making him their first-round pick in 1998, and he turned pro. Two years later, he was named to Team USA for the Summer Olympics in Sydney, Australia, and cried when his club won the gold medal.

Burroughs was brash. Playing in Class A in 1999, he spotted Padres general manager Kevin Towers and yelled, "Hey, K.T.!" In 2002, he was promoted to the Padres and enjoyed a solid year — .286 with 7 home runs. Some called him "the next Tony Gwynn."

Former Red Wings broadcaster Glenn Geffner was doing radio for the Padres when Burroughs made his debut.

"He was just a humble, hard-working kid who didn't take anything for granted," Geffner said.

Geffner's 2-year-old son, Corey, idolized Burroughs, and the two became pals. Last year, when Burroughs returned to the majors with the Diamondbacks, Geffner approached him in the batting cage in Phoenix. "Not only did he know exactly who I was, it took him all of 30 seconds to ask me about Corey," says Geffner, now a radio broadcaster for the Miami Marlins.

A few weeks later, when Geffner and his family waited in Miami to say hello to Burroughs after a game, the player and the now 10-year-old Corey picked up as if it were 2002 all over again.

Burroughs had a great left-handed stroke, but little power for a third baseman. By 2005, he was back in the minors. The Padres traded him to Tampa Bay before the 2006 season. The Rays released him in August. The Mariners signed him before the '07 season and sent him to Triple-A Tacoma.

He played four games, and then simply quit the sport he loved. He told reporters he had lost his passion. But he had found another passion that would send his life into a spiral.

"I began my run," he says. "It was a gradual thing."

But a quick descent. Burroughs had fallen in with the wrong crowd, and drug binges soon became the norm for him. He was, as he told ESPN last year, "knocking at death's door."

"What I was doing, there wasn't any stopping until I was dead or pulled my head out of my (butt)," he says. "That took five years. And the last three were pretty bad."

He partied nightly in Las Vegas, regularly staying out until 4 in the morning. His diet consisted of Slurpees — sometimes eight a day — and burgers and fries.

His parents, Jeff and Debbie, became concerned when Sean's friends said they were worried about him — and they were the ones partying with the former star. His family tried to help, but he shooed them away. He missed two Christmases and one Thanksgiving.

"I told them everything was fine, but it wasn't," he says. "There weren't any off days in my new profession. I used drugs every day. And it just got tiring. I was mentally drained, physically drained and spiritually bankrupt."

Financially, he was fine. He had a home, a car and money. But he was "going insane."

"I would talk to things that weren't around. I thought my house was haunted. I thought my telephone was tapped. I would be up for 8-10 days at a time (without sleep), and paranoia set in."

One day, Burroughs looked in the mirror and didn't recognize the person staring back at him. He weighed about 260 pounds, his hair was a greasy mess, and he had dark bags under his eyes.

"It was time to stop," he says.

And so Sean Burroughs, a millionaire approaching 30, moved back into his bedroom in his parents' house and was given a budget and a curfew. He helped his mother teach her Spanish-speaking first-grade class in Long Beach. He talked baseball nonstop with his famous dad. And he got himself back into shape, working out with Phillies star second baseman Chase Utley, a friend from their Little League days.

"I did it," he says, "with willpower."

Eventually, he yearned to be back in the game he had left.

His agent called around, looking for a tryout invitation. Kevin Towers, the Arizona Diamondbacks general manager and former Padres GM, decided to give his former third baseman a chance.

Burroughs started the 2011 season with Triple-A Reno, but a month later he was back in the majors with a playoff-bound club. He ended up hitting a respectable .273 in 78 games for the Diamondbacks.

He was a free agent in the offseason and signed with the Twins after getting a recommendation from current Wings manager Gene Glynn, Burroughs' coach in Venezuela last winter.

"I knew his story," Glynn says. "I only knew him from the field. But I saw a guy that gave his all 100 percent of the time and had a ton of energy. I thought he could help the Twins."

Burroughs broke camp with the big league club but hit just .118 in 10 games and was optioned to Rochester, where he is often heard before he is seen in the clubhouse.

"He's got a lot of energy and fire," Wings outfielder Brian Dinkelman says. "You know he's there. He keeps us loose."

Burroughs is fluent in the Spanish he learned in high school and loves to chat up the Latino players on his team. In his first trip through the minors, he intentionally roomed with teammates from different cultures. He was once the only male in a yoga class with 25 women — including his mother. He's playing on a last-place club in the minors, but all is well. He talks to his parents a lot (mainly by text; he's not much of a phone person). He has a steady girlfriend. He has a nice apartment.

He has that incredible past. But mostly, he has his future.

"I can't do the things I did when I was younger," he says. "I play more for the love of the game and the camaraderie of teammates.

"It's a cliché, but I've been given a second chance. Baseball is the cherry on top."

The adventure continues.

CAL RIPKEN JR.:
BEFORE THE LEGEND

Published October 6, 2001

You won't believe that the young, fun-loving prankster who played for the Rochester Red Wings in 1981 grew up to be a national baseball icon.

THE 13-YEAR-OLD BAT BOY AND THE 20-YEAR-OLD THIRD BASEMAN followed a daily routine during that summer of 1981. They would arrive at Silver Stadium in Rochester by 1 p.m. — six hours before the first pitch. The third baseman brought his own lunch, which he would quickly eat; then he'd announce, "Let's go out and get after it." The two would then head out to the field. The bat boy, Chris Costello, would hit countless ground balls to the player. And then the third baseman, a prospect named Cal Ripken Jr., would reciprocate for his young friend. "We'd be the only two people out on the field except for (longtime groundskeeper) Dick Sierens watering the dirt," Costello says with a laugh.

Ripken is a baseball icon now. But back then he was merely a highly regarded minor leaguer. Selected in the second round of the 1978 draft by the Baltimore Orioles, he joined the Red Wings as the organization's No. 1 prospect in April 1981.

"We knew we were going to draft Junior," says Tom Giordano, the former Baltimore Orioles scouting and farm director. "But we didn't know if we would draft him as a pitcher or a shortstop. He was so good at both in high school."

On draft night, Giordano asked Cal Sr., Baltimore's longtime coach, for guidance.

"I called him and said 'Cal, we're going to draft your son. Is he a pitcher or a shortstop?'" Giordano recalls. "And Senior said, 'Make him a shortstop. He wants to play every day.'"

And play every day he did, for 16 years and 2,632 consecutive games. He switched from shortstop to third in the minors, and then

went back to short in a now-famous move designed by Orioles manager Earl Weaver. At first, Ripken wondered if he had made a big
mistake. He was playing rookie ball in Bluefield, West Virginia, with
a center-field wall that was ridiculously short at just 365 feet. He hit
no home runs in 239 at-bats that season. Ripken hit eight homers
at Double-A Charlotte, North Carolina in 1980 (playing in all 144
games) and homered in the Red Wings' season opener on Friday,
April 10, 1981, a 6-5 win over Pawtucket in 13 innings at Silver.

Ripken wasn't around for the end of that game, however. Wings
manager Doc Edwards pulled him in favor of left-handed-hitting
Tom Chism in the ninth inning, and Chism hit a game-tying single.

"I understood," Ripken told reporters afterward, which
prompted *Democrat and Chronicle* columnist Greg Boeck to write,
"This is no normal 20-year-old."

Years later, Ripken admits he was mystified by the move.

"I couldn't help thinking, 'Wait a minute! I hit a home run in my
last at-bat!'" he said.

Ripken had a terrific work ethic even then. In addition to spending time with Costello, he and roommate Floyd Rayford would
throw 100 batting practice pitches to each other before the rest of the
team showed. But Ripken also had fun.

"He was one of the gang," says Costello, now the media relations director for the Tampa Bay Devil Rays. "We used sticky letters
to spell out players' names above their lockers, and Cal would put
extra letters on to change the names."

Ripken's favorite "victim" was teammate John Shelby. He would
put shaving cream in Shelby's jockstrap and nail his shoes to the
clubhouse ceiling. The good-natured Shelby would return the favor.
Kevin Johnston, the Wings' clubhouse attendant that year, remembered how Ripken's mischief got him in cold water one night.

"Cal and another teammate were the only players left at 2 a.m.,"
Johnston recalled, "and as a joke my brother Steve and I filled an ice
bucket with cold water and dumped it on them."

While Ripken hosed Steve down in the bathroom, Kevin put
Ripken's clothes on as a prank. Ripken jumped out and dumped a
bucket of water on Johnston, soaking his own clothes. He ended up

driving to his apartment in Greece wearing only his damp sneakers and tennis shorts.

Ripken had played all 114 games at Rochester, when he finally was called up to Baltimore on August 8, immediately after the major league players' strike ended.

He languished on the bench behind Doug DeCinces in Baltimore and had no plate appearances after September 4 "because we were in a pennant race and I guess Earl Weaver didn't trust me." He finished the year at a dismal 5-for-39 (.128) with no RBI — and no confidence.

The rest is history. DeCinces eventually was traded and Ripken was moved to shortstop, where he won American League MVP honors and led the Orioles to the 1983 World Series title. He won another MVP award in 1991, and broke Lou Gehrig's revered record of 2,130 consecutive games four years after that. For a long time, Ripken had a consecutive innings streak. When Red Wings legend Joe Altobelli managed the Orioles from 1983-85, Ripken was the only shortstop he used. Inning after inning after inning.

"At the end of every year I'd tell him, 'Now Cal, next year you're going to sit for a few,'" Altobelli recalls. "But next year would come and he'd play every inning of every game."

Altobelli finally asked Ripken what made him so determined to play no matter the score or situation.

"He told me, 'Joe, when I went up in '81 I had to sit on the bench and I hated it. I promised myself that if I ever got in, I'd never come out.'"

Ripken returned to Rochester 13 times for exhibitions, including visits to Frontier Field in 1997 and '99, when he signed hundreds of autographs. Ripken enjoyed playing for the Wings, but he loved eating wings even more. Chicken wings, that is.

"I remember he came back here in 1989 and was taken out of the game in the sixth inning," says Terry "Thurm" Costello, Chris' brother and the Red Wings' longtime visitors' clubhouse attendant. "He put on his street clothes, borrowed my assistant's car and drove over to the Garage Door (a nearby restaurant) with teammate Craig Worthington.

"He was there until the end of the game, eating wings. All the people at Silver who wanted his autograph would have had a better shot if they'd gone to the Garage Door that night!"

Four years later, the Orioles cancelled their trip to Rochester to make up a game with the Chicago White Sox. Costello answered the phone in the visitors' clubhouse and spoke with Orioles trainer Jamie Reed.

"Cal was really looking forward to coming to Rochester and having chicken wings," Reed said.

The trainer then asked Costello if he would fly to Baltimore for a game, spend a night in a nice hotel, and fly back to Rochester the next day — all at Ripken's expense. All he had to do was bring a bundle of wings.

"I would have loved it," Costello says, "but we were starting a homestand and I couldn't get off."

Ripken eventually got on the line, too, but Costello said no.

"He was OK with it," Costello recalls, "but he was disappointed. This was before chicken wings were sold at every pizza place in the country. Coming to Rochester was a big deal."

In 1997, the Orioles played at Frontier Field before taking a charter flight to Minnesota. At Ripken's request, they also took 1,000 wings from Pontillo's Pizzeria with them.

How was Cal as a tipper?

"Without getting into specifics, I'll say he was the best," Costello says.

His generosity extended beyond his wallet. At some point during each exhibition, Ripken and Costello would lock themselves in an office with a couple of beers and dozens of baseballs.

"He had a system where I would hand him a ball and he'd sign it and hand it back to me, at which point I'd hand him another ball," Costello says. "He was signing for the Red Wings players, the staff and others."

Ripken said he designed the system because so many opposing players in the big leagues would ask for his autograph. On the last day of every road trip, he would sit down with the clubby and fulfill each request.

"It's amazing enough to get that much admiration from your peers where they're asking for your autograph," Terry Costello says. "The fact that it happened so much that he had to develop a system . . . well, that says all you need to say about Cal Ripken Jr."

Once, Ripken asked Costello if he needed anything. The clubhouse attendant shook his head, saying, "I'm not a collector."

Ripken laughed. "That's a refreshing attitude," he said.

EPILOGUE

So what became of these people—the famous and the not-so-famous?

In 2007, **Cal Ripken Jr.** went on to earn a first-ballot induction into the Baseball Hall of Fame. I was there that torrid July day in Cooperstown, New York, along with 75,000 other fans. Ripken remains busy as a speaker, an author, an owner (he owns the short-season, appropriately-named Aberdeen IronBirds baseball team) and a major-league baseball analyst for TBS Sports.

Jim Nantz continues his dream job as the voice (and face) of CBS Sports and lives in a house overlooking famed Pebble Beach Golf Course in California. **Abby Wambach** is still going strong in her 30s, and in October 2013 she married Sarah Huffman in Hawaii. With every international goal Wambach scores, she breaks her own world record.

Bob Ward remains the St. John Fisher athletic director as he nears age 70. He still works out six days a week. **Mike Neer** retired from the University of Rochester men's basketball team in 2010, stayed away one season, and guided Hobart College in Geneva, New York to three straight NCAA Division III Tournaments. In July 2014, now a grandfather, he retired again. He says this time he means it.

Bill O'Rourke Sr. passed away in 2006 at age 82. Among his visitors at the nursing home were the 16 players on his son's Webster Thomas varsity team, who signed a basketball and brought it to him. **Bill O'Rourke Jr.** retired from coaching in 2013 at age 65, ending a 63-year era in which he or his dad coached a Webster varsity team: 811 wins from 1950-2013. "I'll miss coaching forever," O'Rourke Jr. said.

Jenn Suhr got her gold, winning the pole vault at the 2012 Summer Olympics in London. **Chris Colabello** turned down a $1 million contract to play baseball in South Korea in 2014, with no guarantees of making the Minnesota Twins if he rejected the offer.

But he did reject it, made the Twins and was the American League's Co-Player of the Month in April, along with Anaheim superstar Josh Hamilton. However, Colabello was demoted twice to the Triple-A Rochester Red Wings, putting his future with the Twins — but not baseball — in limbo. "I want to wear a uniform for a team, any team, as long as I can," he said. He started the 2015 season in the Toronto Blue Jays system.

Jonathon Lillis came tantalizingly close to making the 2014 Winter Olympics but was bypassed by the selection committee. He's already looking forward to the 2018 Olympic Games in South Korea, thankful to be alive to pursue his dream.

"Part-Time Joe" (**Joe Vicario**) was thrilled to remain part of the Rochester Institute of Technology hockey programs as they opened the new Gene Polisseni Center in October 2014. He's on track to graduate in 2015 and hopes to stay on with the hockey teams. "It will be hard for me not to be a part of it," he says and adds that he is thinking of going for his master's degree in sports management.

Bobby Greco worked at Jim Kelly's 2014 football camp as a senior division coach and was invited to the Pro Football Hall of Fame induction ceremony and party for former Buffalo Bills receiver Andre Reed in Canton, Ohio. His dad's musical act, The Bob Greco Band, played at the induction party.

Bobby Grich founded the Anaheim Angels Alumni Association in 2002 and still works for his old club in various roles. When he's not doing that, he's golfing. In 2014, he was reunited with **Don Baylor,** who was hired as the Angels' hitting coach.

Seth Johnston played only one season for the Brockport men's basketball team, but has been a Golden Eagles assistant coach since 2007. **Erin Muir** is now Erin Etsler, a real estate agent and pro fitness contestant. She lives in Churchville, New York, with McKennzie — now a high school junior who plays travel soccer — and sons Tommy and Jimmy.

Sean Burroughs spent the 2014 baseball season with the Bridgeport Bluefish, a team in the independent Atlantic League. He was far removed from the major leagues, but he was having a blast. **Charlotte Reardon**, who ran like the wind despite her battle with cystic fibrosis — graduated from the Harvard School of Public Health in 2012 and works as a management consultant in New York City. She still runs three to five miles, three times a week . . . and her health is great, with a dramatic reduction in her coughing and lung congestion. "It still takes work to keep it up and stay healthy," she says, "but not wanting to use my vacation to get treatments has been a huge motivator to stay on track."

Phil Roof, now in his mid-70s, continues to be a special coach for the Minnesota Twins at spring training. The baseball-loving father and daughter team — **Ed and Mary Blasko** — were a constant presence at Rochester Red Wings games again in 2014. But they were there with heavy hearts. Ed's wife of 59 years, Donna — Mary's beloved mother — died, surrounded by her loving family, on March 22, 2014. **Murph Shapiro** has retired from his jobs as athletic director and basketball official. He misses Hawaii. **Howard Bingham** continues to stay active with or without his famous best friend. His book, *Muhammad Ali's Greatest Fight: Cassius Clay vs. The United States of America,* was turned into an HBO movie.

Cancer survivor **Kristine Pierce** is now Kristine Pierce-Brassie. A stay-at-home mom heavily involved in volunteer work in her Mendon, New York, community, she has been cancer-free since 1997 and no longer needs regular checkups. She and husband David are the parents of four children – born in 2003, 2004, 2005 and 2006. "Not bad for someone they said wouldn't be able to have kids," Kristine says with a laugh. After the first one, Kristine told David she wanted 12 kids. He met her a third of the way. She couldn't be happier.

The people profiled in this book remain not only a part of my career, but a part of my memories. All enriched me and inspired me in different ways. All stepped outside the game to share their stories with me, which allowed me to share them with you. It is a gift that keeps on giving.

ABOUT THE AUTHOR

Jim Mandelaro has been writing for the Rochester (New York) *Democrat and Chronicle* since 1986. He is a three-time winner of the New York State Associated Press award for outstanding sports feature writing, a two-time recipient of the Rochester Press-Radio Club Sportswriter of the Year Award and a member of the Frontier Field Walk of Fame. He covered the Rochester Red Wings from 1991 to 2014 and co-authored the books *Silver Seasons: The Story of the Rochester Red Wings* and *Silver Seasons and a New Frontier* with Scott Pitoniak. The St. John Fisher College graduate lives in Fairport, New York, with his wife, Kerri, and their children, Matthew and Sophia.

INDEX

Page numbers in italics indicate illustrations.

COLOPHON

DESIGN
Marnie Soom

TYPEFACES
Palatino Linotype and Trade Gothic

PRINTING AND BINDING
Thomson-Shore
Dexter, MI

 **green** **press** INITIATIVE

RIT Press is committed to preserving ancient forests and natural resources. We elected to print this title on 30% post consumer recycled paper, processed chlorine free. As a result, for this printing, we have saved:

3 Trees (40' tall and 6-8" diameter)
2 Million BTUs of Total Energy
222 Pounds of Greenhouse Gases
1,202 Gallons of Wastewater
80 Pounds of Solid Waste

RIT Press made this paper choice because our printer, Thomson-Shore, Inc., is a member of Green Press Initiative, a nonprofit program dedicated to supporting authors, publishers, and suppliers in their efforts to reduce their use of fiber obtained from endangered forests.

For more information, visit www.greenpressinitiative.org

Environmental impact estimates were made using the Environmental Defense Paper Calculator. For more information visit: www.papercalculator.org.